Learning the Mysteries

by

Letty Lincoln

Cartledge Publishers
Bemis Printing Co.

St. Helens, Oregon

Learning the Mysteries

Contents

Introduction   1

Chapter 1 What do you Mean, Mystery School   6

Beginnings   7

Participants   15

The Teacher   17

Roots of the Mystery Teachings   20

Setting   23

Chapter 2 Holakuna Knowledge   28

Basic Concepts   28

Life Style   30

Nature of Life and the World   31

Elana's Teaching Procedures   35

Problems for Observation   41

First Weekend: Exorcism, Death, and Qasi Resurrection   42

Building a New Reality   49

Chapter 3 The Low Self   51

The Second Weekend: Water and the Second Chakra   51

Contention   54

The Third Weekend: Amon-Ra and the High Will   60

Issues   67

Chapter 4 Entering the Middle Self: The Holy Family   70

The Fourth Weekend: Heart and Bonding   70

Chapter 5 Bonding and Changing   80

The Fifth Weekend: The Throat Chakra   80

Learning the Mysteries

Vision Quest Meditation 88

The Sixth Weekend: Sound, Dismemberment and Change 92

Holy Family Business 98

Chapter 6 Embodying the High Self 101

The Seventh Weekend: Third Eye, Clear Consciousness 101

The Eighth Weekend: Crown Chakra 110

Chapter 7 Everything you Know is Wrong 121

The Ninth Weekend: Entering the Void 121

Like Little Children 132

Chapter 8 Healing, Learning, Transcending 135

Holakuna Healing, Yoga and Shamanism 136

Participant Views of Holakuna Knowledge 140

Participant Learning Experience 141

Transcendence 151

Chapter 9 Self, Mind and Revitalization 153

Experiencing the Holakuna Reality 154

Mind outside Self 156

The Urge to Transcend 157

Revitalization 159

A Crisis in Meaning 162

Is Holakuna a Religion or Cult? 167

Glossary 169

References 175

Acknowledgements 182

List of Illustrations

Fig. 2.1 The Chakra Minds and Three Selves 36

Fig. 5.1 Initiates Head out into the Desert on their Quests. 90

List of Tables

Table.1.1 Months of Holakuna Mystery School Weekend Sessions. . . .14

Table 2.1 Correspondences of Holakuna Elements, Faculties, Chakras,

And Colors to Directions 32

Introduction

I first encountered Huna during the 1960s in popular books by Frank Edwards, radio and TV journalist. His references led me to the writings of Max Freedom Long and Serge King, who claimed to have uncovered this hidden esoteric knowledge. Huna was said to be an ancient secret tradition dating back to pre-dynastic ancient Egypt or to the fabled Atlantis. According to this narrative, either following or preceding some cataclysmic disruption, an ancient, but advanced civilization sent out a contingent of specially trained teachers to spread over the world, bearing the important secret and empowering knowledge their civilization possessed. This knowledge was to be preserved as each teacher passed it on to just one well-chosen lineage bearer for succeeding generations. Hence the discipline could be preserved until advanced civilization arose once more and humankind was ready to receive it.

During the 20th century lineages were supposedly uncovered in Central Asia, Hawaii (where they were said to comprise a secret society among the Kahunas or priests), and North Africa. The authors of these books claimed to have contacted or been trained by bearers of such esoteric lineages.

The idea intrigued me, but while open to considering this notion, I was always skeptical. The survival of such lineages for millennia seemed unlikely, given the sorts of upheavals that had occurred. Changes in environment or culture frequently require that secret beliefs and practices be revised or reinvented in order to make sense in new contexts. Thus

1

ethnic ancestral secrets are sometimes not as ancient or unchanged as adherents believe them to be. Furthermore the thesis of ancient secret knowledge passed on by a few of the chosen is suspect, simply because it appears countless times in popular literature, making it seem more the stuff of myth, founded on some obscure truth, rather than history. Consider Hilton's *The Lost Horizon* or the literary works of Carlos Castaneda.

During the 1980s I became involved in a small study group in Morgantown, West Virginia associated with the human potential teachings of Jean Houston, a psychologist and scholar who founded a mystery school featuring the esoteric practices of ancient Greece. There the story of Huna surfaced again and my interest was once more piqued. A few years later I moved to Eugene, Oregon where I discovered that Huna or Kahuna teachers were offering workshops. I attended a beginning class offered by Regena, an initiate and teacher. Subsequently I took two more Huna classes.

Chapter one of this book explains how my anthropological study of a Huna mystery school began. As sole researcher I was a participant-apprentice, entering the school as a full participant to take part in all student activities and experience while pursuing my academic research. Ethnographic field methods included: attending all sessions of the school and doing observation during lectures, question and answer periods, group dialogues, and recesses, as well as interviewing eleven participants in depth at times and places outside the school.

I promised Elana, the mystery school lineage-bearer and teacher, as did all participants, that I would not reveal the content of initiations, mantras, and practices to anyone outside the mystery school. In writing up research I tried to keep this promise by discussing the forms and purposes of initiations and practices in very general terms. I changed words for all the mantras, sacred forces, and spirit beings, except those most commonly known to the West through the patois spoken by adherents to ancient Egyptian culture, yoga, Buddhism, spiritualism, or shamanism. I concentrated on group interaction, individual learning process and the experience of mystery school, mailing chapters of my dissertation to Elana as I finished them, in accordance with our agreement, (Although unfortunately, through some mishap she did not receive several chapters.)

I had been fooling myself believing everything written would be acceptable to Elana. After reading the completed draft of the ethnography, she accused me of revealing all her teachings in my manuscript and begged me not to publish. I had not thought revealing such general content as the organizational framework of the curriculum (by far not all her teaching, but perhaps the core of it) broke our initial agreement. It was necessary to provide something of the type of material and experiences participants encountered in order to discuss their learning.

Above all, Elana was my friend and my teacher. I simply could not betray her by publishing the study against her wishes. Hence I did not seek publication, even though my dissertation committee advised me to do so. In consequence I have been called to task professionally. Nevertheless at the time I felt the opportunity to publish would probably develop years later.

Elana passed away in 1999 at the age of 53. At the time I was heavily engaged in writing the ethnography of an American ethnic learning circle. It is only recently that I have been able to attend to revising the mystery school ethnography for publication. I believe that this is an auspicious time for its release.

This book stems from my exploratory ethnographic study of the Holakuna[1] Mystery School: exploratory in the sense that it investigated an institution never before studied. I examined individual participants' experiences both in the mystery school setting and in mundane life related to their MS participation. My research questions were: "What happens at mystery school?" and "What do participants experience in their lives in conjunction with mystery school attendance?" I wanted to know what was being taught and how students and teacher were interacting. A secondary line of inquiry investigated the significance of Elana's approach to teaching and learning.

Chapter one explains how Elana became lineage-bearer for life mysteries and how I approached this study. Chapter two presents basic ideas participants learned in classes required before attending mystery school and my impressions at the first weekend session. Chapters three through seven chronicle the mystery school unfolding over a year and a half. Later, as data from interviews and observations were sorted six developmental categories important to participants and teacher emerged: healing, knowing, transcendence, synchronicity, opening, and learning at the cellular level. (By this I mean perceived physiological changes as a direct result of practice.) These are discussed and interpreted in chapter 8, drawing on participant interviews and conversations.

Chapter 9 explores the broader meaning of Elana's Mystery School in the contexts of the late 1980s. First I compare and contrast its beliefs and practices with those of concurrent yoga and shamanism (or neo-shamanism), then examine social issues the school seemed to address. The book concludes with the global implications of MS participants' learning and transcendence.

My purpose for this volume is not to publish a scholarly rendition. Although the ethnography served well in its time, this current telling is meant to present simply an introductory, experiential look into the Holakuna Mystery School for the discerning reader.

Note

1.   Holakuna is a term I invented to replace the actual name of Elana's school and discipline.

Chapter 1: What do you Mean, Mystery School?

When I first proposed to do this ethnography, many of my colleagues in anthropology and education had never heard of a mystery school. They asked me "What do you mean by mystery school?" Some of them assumed I was keeping the name of a public school I intended to study a mystery in order to protect the identity of its students and teachers.

Wrong! This was an exploratory ethnography of the Holakuna Mystery School for adults, exploratory in the sense that at that time, to the best of my knowledge, no social scientist had studied a contemporary American mystery school. Such venues were and still are, by their very nature, secret. Students at the school were required to promise not to reveal, teach, or publish any of the mantras, initiations, or practices learned in MS training, which is typical of mystery schools at any time. They also agreed not to tell outsiders where and when the school met, or who attended.

Mystery schools were an uncommon social phenomenon in 1987 when my research began. Jean Houston, psychologist and author of *The Possible Human* (1982) and *The Search for the Beloved* (1987) created such a school to impart her "sacred psychology" in New York during the early 1980s. According to Houston, sacred psychology reveals one's previously untapped reservoirs of personal richness, depth, strength, and mystery. (1987)

Gay Gaer Luce, author of *Body Time* (1971), offered Nine Gates of Mystery, also referred to as a mystery school by its graduates. Luce's school, meeting in California, revealed secret teachings of nine different religious traditions, featuring guest teachers from each of them. In 2013 the Jean Houston Mystery School and Nine Gates of Mystery were still active. It is much easier now to find mystery schools through the internet. My web search turned up at least 13 enterprises similar to the Holakuna School, teaching ancient Egyptian and/or new age concepts.

Beginnings

When I arrived for the first weekend session of the Holakuna Mystery School in 1987, my situation was similar to that of an anthropologist entering a newly contacted native village, in that I did not know what to expect. On the other hand it was quite different from the classic anthropologist's situation because the school had not existed before that day. I was on an equal footing with other participants in constructing the culture of the school. Holakuna Mystery School was my village, a phenomenon of my American culture as yet unknown to its expectant students.

Still, like the classic anthropologist who had seen neighboring villages, I knew something about this school because I had attended three Holakuna preliminary workshops and some other smaller shamanistic and spiritual groups. I knew that initiation, visualization, and ritual would be part of the mystery school experience. I knew basic precepts of the Holakuna belief system and their terminology. I understood that the Holakuna version of reality differed markedly from the typical Westerner's notions of what is real and what is possible.

I had heard again of the Huna or Kahuna tradition in the early 1980s while participating in workshops based on Jean Houston's sacred psychology organized and taught by a woman who had attended the Jean Houston Mystery School. This source informed me once more that Huna, or Kahuna is purported to be an ancient, secret body of teaching dating back to pre-dynastic Egypt or before, passed down through the ages by lineages of teachers whose forerunners migrated from Egypt to locations scattered around the globe. (Hawaii, Central Asia, and North Africa are designated in Huna literature.) [1]

Information about these purported lineages of esoteric teachers could be found in books popular among new age readers at the time, such as those by Max Freedom Long and Serge King, advocates for two separate Huna, or Kahuna lineages. Max Freedom Long (1890-1971) founded Huna Research, Inc. and is author of *Recovering the Ancient*

Magic (1936) published in England, *Secret Science Behind Miracles*, and thirteen other publications about Huna. After Long's death Huna Research, Inc. continued to publish Huna books by other authors. Serge King has taught Kahuna workshops in California and Hawaii and is the author of *Mastering Your Hidden Self: A Guide to the Kahuna Way* and four other books about the tradition.

Huna and Kahuna are names registered as trademarks by teachers of what is generally believed to be the same tradition as Elana's. Huna Research, Inc. of Missouri has registered the name Huna as their trademark. Kahuna is a Hawaiian term for a priest, sorcerer, magician, minister, healer, or expert in any field. Westerners using this term in other ways may be accused of appropriating native Hawaiian culture. Mystery school participants used the terms Huna and Kahuna when referring specifically to the teachers, practitioners, and to the mystery school itself. They also used the words as adjectives. Because Elana, the mystery school teacher and lineage-bearer, could not legally use these terms, she experimented with several different names for her lineage. In this writing I refer to Elana's teachings as Holakuna. Here Kahuna and Huna are considered native terms, generic names for the legendary esoteric tradition. I use Holakuna to refer to Elana's lineage, representing but one branch of the alleged tradition.

After moving to Eugene, Oregon in 1985, I noticed an advertisement for Holakuna classes on a bulletin board at a natural food store. Later a teacher in the public school system where I served as a student teacher supervisor told me about the Holakuna class she was attending. During 1986 and 1987 I went to two of these classes offered by the teacher Regina, (All personal names used in this work are pseudonyms.) Later I took a class taught by Elana, Regena's teacher. During that class Elana informed us that her own mystery school was about to open. At that time I was considering sites for my dissertation ethnography in anthropology and education at University of Oregon, hoping to explore the relationship between religious based education and student learning. The notion of studying Elana's school hovered in the back of my mind but didn't seem possible, given the secrecy involved, not to mention perceived boundaries of my academic field. Hence, in a planning meeting with my dissertation advisor and mentor, studying Elana's school was at the bottom of my list of possibilities. Surprisingly, my advisor urged me to pursue the mystery school study.

Under his guidance and with Regina's support I wrote to Elana in the fall of 1987, enrolling for the school and asking permission to do the anthropological study as a full participant. From the beginning I was convinced that full participation as an initiate was the only possible way I would be allowed to do this research, since only those fully committed are allowed to be present during mystery school sessions.

Two weeks later, on October 10, I received a phone call from Elana. She welcomed me to her Mystery School and expressed interest regarding my proposed research. I assured her that I did not want to analyze anything about mystery school, but was interested in exploring experiences in the participants' lives, which they might perceive as being related to the school. I also told Elana that the concept of spirit had not received much attention in educational research and literature, and that this study would at least introduce "spirit" into the literature of education in a small way. I explained that I was interested in doing an ethnographic study, a genre of research that does not isolate variables and scrutinize their relationship or search for cause and effect. Rather, I told her, ethnography is a holistic approach to the study of culture, looking at such things as group interaction and learning.

Elana gave her verbal approval for the study. In fact she expressed excitement at the prospect. She liked the idea that a scholarly record of the school would be made, saying that I would serve as the historian of the group. She also said she wanted to cite my research in her publications, and I could cite her writings. Elana indicated that she looked forward to reading my findings on the students' perspective of their experience with the school.

In this initial approval Elana placed some limitations on my ethnographic activities during the weekend mystery school sessions. She insisted that students not be told of the impending research until the fourth weekend in April of 1988, following the "opening of the heart" and "the forming of the holy family." I was permitted to record sessions and take notes, but during the first four weekends the participants were not to know of the proposed ethnography. She also asked me not to conduct interviews at any time during the weekend sessions. Elana felt that such overt activity during the sessions would be disruptive. All interviews were to be conducted outside the mystery school. Sitting apart from the group to observe from a vantage point was also forbidden. She indicated that all participants would be busy. There would be no time for these activities during the sessions. This proved to be correct.

At the time Elana gave her approval I did not realize (I was told later by an informant close to her,) that she referred all decisions regarding mystery school to the *neters* through prayer and psychic channeling. Neters are personifications of the universal principles of existence. In Elana's version of Holakuna the neters most often evoked take the form of ancient Egyptian gods and goddesses. Neters are more than archetypes. They are principles active in the universe. For example Thoth personifies thought, a force or principle active in the world. Although depicted as male and female, neters are actually androgynous. Elana taught that in terms of their principles and functions they blend into each other. Ultimately they are all one.

For the first four weekends I tape-recorded Elana's teaching sessions and her dialogue with participants, and took notes. I was uncertain as to the limits of my note taking and questions. I was not to take data without the informants knowing about the study, but what constituted data? I was also afraid of revealing my extra purpose for being in mystery school before the appointed time. This might jeopardize my acceptance among the participants, which seemed to be complete, and compromise Elana's good will. Consequently, I resorted to taking notes while tape-recording lecture sessions, including dialogue between participants and teacher. I excluded personal material expressed in the group. Thus much material was lost that might have been useful after attaining participant consent. It was uncomfortable to sit there as an ethnographer, letting all that pertinent information go by, but I thought it was the ethical course of action. I kept a journal throughout mystery school after leaving each weekend session. In it I wrote down my own personal experience as a participant.

Saturday morning during the fourth session Elana introduced the possibility of the ethnographic study to the participants. She made it clear she endorsed the study, emphasizing that this research might be a means by which the concept of "spirit" would be introduced into the literature of professional education. I then explained to the group that this ethnography would not involve experiments, causality, or isolating and manipulating variables, but that ethnographers conduct dialogues with informants through which they hope to accrue knowledge as the informants themselves have constructed it. I told them there would be no interference with the school sessions. Participant observation would mean the ethnographer would sit among them and take notes, as I had already been doing. (Many other participants took notes and recorded lectures.) Interviews would be arranged outside mystery school.

The participants approved the study. No disapproval was voiced and subsequently twenty-seven of the forty participants signed informed consent forms, agreeing to be interviewed. Elana's restrictions may have

Table 1.1 Months of Holakuna Mystery School Weekend Sessions

Session	Month	Year
1.	November	1987
2.	December	1987
3.	January	1988
4.	March	1988
5.	April	1988
6.	June	1988
7.	September	1988
8.	October	1988
9.	December	1988
10.	March	1989

curtailed some field activities but they also they also kept the research From interfering with the mystery school process, allowing me to document its unfolding.

Participants

Forty-four adults were enrolled at the first session in November of 1987, having made a commitment to attend all ten sessions at a cost of $400.00 per session, which included room and board. This figure is comparable with the cost of other spiritual and shamanic workshops at the time. Of the forty-four one man never attended. A forty-fifth, a man, was admitted at the second session and never returned. One woman was seriously injured in a traffic accident after the third session and did not come back. One man dropped mystery school after the fifth session because of a skin condition seemingly related to his attendance. Another woman attended irregularly before dropping out. After the fifth weekend one woman was asked in a letter from another female participant representing a small vocal group to either leave or change her behavior. She decided to drop out.[2] One man dropped mystery school after the fifth session because of a skin condition seemingly related to his attendance. The school ended with thirty-seven active participants, including nine men.

An additional man attending was Larry, the business manager of Elana's Holakuna teaching organization. During mystery school he acted as a combined teacher's aide and manager, negotiating with conference center staff, organizing materials, and running errands for Elana or delegating others to do so. Larry also participated with students in school activities, particularly practices and personal sharing sessions.

During sharing participants told the group about personal blocks that they were attempting to work through, or "get past" in order to continue their spiritual development. For example, during the first four weekend sessions the passing of Elana's shaman staff was observed on Friday evenings. Participants sat in a circle and passed the staff from hand to hand. Whoever held it had to tell the truth, and tell what he or she least wanted the others to know about themselves. (See Chapter 3.)

The majority of participants were in their forties and fifties. The youngest, a woman, was a twenty-nine year old health care professional. The oldest, also a woman, was seventy-four and a widow. Most people attending mystery school were successful middle-aged professionals from middle class backgrounds. Many pursued careers in psychology, counseling, nursing, or physical therapy. Marriage, guidance, abuse, and sex counseling were well represented among them. There were several educators and three professional musicians, part of the same new age combo. Of these, the female vocalist also taught music to children. There was one herbalist, one itinerant shaman woman, a business man, two lawyers, computer program designer, and several homemakers. Most of the participants came from the West Coast, many from California. Five were from the Pacific Northwest, four from the Midwest or Southwest. One man traveled from Western Europe to attend.

The Teacher

During the course of several mystery school sessions Elana told participants a little about her childhood. According to Elana, her family had a strong tradition of shamanism, particularly on her mother's side. They were also devotees of Paramahansa Yogananda, author of *Autobiography of a Yogi*, an East Indian guru who came to America in 1920 and by 1925 had founded the Self Realization Fellowship/Yogoda Society, headquartered in Los Angeles (Yogananda 1998). Someone prominent in the Self Realization Fellowship predicted before Elana's birth that she would be a significant spiritual teacher. Consequently her family moved to a wilderness location designated to be the place where this expected spiritual leader should be born. During Elana's childhood it was not uncommon for members of her immediate family to sense and discuss spirit phenomena. Her mother, who was well versed in esoteric knowledge, provided support for Elana during her early psychic experiences.

In adulthood Elana received the secret teachings from two lineage bearers, a Huna woman from Eastern Europe and a Kahuna man from Hawaii. She told her students she met her first teacher, the woman here called Marta, when she approached Marta to have a horoscope chart prepared. Purportedly Marta looked at Elana's astrological birth chart and said, "I have been *vaiting* for you." Elana's chart indicated that she was Marta's Huna successor. Thereafter, according to Elana and some of my informants, Elana moved in with Marta and lived with her for two years, during which time she received the teachings and initiations of Marta's lineage. Elana said she had many notebooks filled with the material taught by Marta. She has also told mystery school participants that Marta was a strange old woman, difficult to get along with at times. During her apprenticeship, Elana often doubted the power and validity of the teaching she received from her mentors, Marta and Albert.

Marta introduced Elana to the Hawaiian-trained Albert, whom she had met fifteen years previously. According to Elana, most of her close friends disliked Albert, who became her lover as well as her teacher. Unlike many spiritual disciplines, Holakuna encourages its practitioners to be sexually active, although this decision and the matter of sexual orientation are left up to the individual. The friends said Albert was reclusive and selfish. Some of Marta's other students tried to influence Elana to sever ties with Albert. Eventually Albert disappeared without warning, much as he had appeared in the local psychic community.

In 1986, before I had thought of doing this ethnography, but after I had attended a preliminary Holakuna class, I made the acquaintance of a man who told me he had known Marta personally, but had not known Elana. Although he had attended one of Marta's classes in which she taught psychic technics, he did not know of the Huna tradition per se. He remembered that every time he went to see Marta there was a young woman "always hanging around" at Marta's house. His description of this woman fits that of Elana's photograph at the time (the mid 1970s). He corroborated Elana's description of Marta as a stubborn, single-minded old woman.

On June 11, 1989 I met a woman who knew Elana and had studied with Marta during the time Elana was also living and studying with her (the early 1970s). This woman had known Albert. She said that Albert did not initially impress her as a great spiritual teacher. He was attractive, short, countrified, and he "appreciated women." She took a class from Albert. His teaching did not impress her as much as his healing power, demonstrated when he did a spiritual healing on a member of her family who suffered nerve damage. During the healing the afflicted leg began to jerk and quiver. What this informant remembered most about Albert was what she termed "his energy." She said that his energy was still with her. In addition to her Holakuna training, Elana had studied Tibetan Buddhism and participated in Nine Gates Mystery School training. She was also quite knowledgeable in other spiritual traditions and topics. She had made an extensive study of Egyptian religion, customs, and language. She was also well versed in current humanistic psychological therapy and counseling techniques, especially Neuro-Linguistic Programming, a form of therapy developed by Richard Bandler and John Grinder in the late1970s. (Bandler and Grinder 1982)

Elana spoke articulately about new age philosophy and of modern scientific research in many fields, especially quantum physics, psychology, and medicine. At the time of the mystery school she was an attractive woman in early middle age. She wore stylish, youthful, natural fabric clothes and accessories, used make-up, had a fashionable hairstyle, and looked the successful professional or businesswoman. From our first meeting she impressed me as a kind, open, and loving individual. At the same time, Elana was a private person. Larry, her business manager, protected her during interims between mystery school sessions to such an extent that participants complained it was difficult to contact Elana when they needed her. Because of the demands of those wanting to spend time with Elana, it was hard to have a long conversation with her during breaks at mystery school. Conversations were usually cut short when she moved on to the next person waiting to speak with her. Those who persisted were able to arrange a personal meeting or phone conversation between mystery school weekends.

Roots of the Mystery Teachings

While it was promoted as Huna or Kahuna knowledge, two other separate bodies of teachings influenced the MS curriculum, namely the human potential movement and the so-called New Age of the 1970s and 1980s. Elana and the participants themselves related these pursuits to the Holakuna tradition.

The Holakuna Tradition

The existence of a body of spiritual teachings promulgated by persons calling themselves Hunas or Kahunas was a concurrent phenomenon in Western culture. Whether or not Marta and Albert's teaching sprang from the ancient roots claimed by these teachers is a question beyond the scope of this ethnography. In the following chapters

20

I will describe the Holakuna teaching in some depth. Here I wish to place it in a recognizable frame.

Human Potential Movement and the New Age

Mystery school participants sought a variety of benefits through their involvement with Holakuna, including: personal healing, increased professional healing ability, spiritual advancement, increased extrasensory perception, and material and social success. Their quest parallels the human potential movement of the 1970s, composed of people who wanted to expand human possibility by first transforming themselves. Adherents pursued possibilities of greater body awareness and function; sharper, extended sense, personal insight, and deeper, more fluent communication with others. They sought to develop spiritual awareness, to surpass their everyday notion of self, and, for some, to pursue oneness with the universe.

Human potential movement adherents employed transpersonal techniques to achieve an expanded sense of self and expanded consciousness. Jean Houston's writing and teaching at the time is strongly identified with the human potential movement. (1982)

Means for increasing one's potential included encounter groups, Gestalt Therapy, Awareness Training, Rolfing, Reiki, Transactional Analysis, sensory awareness, Primal Therapy, Bioenergetics, massage, Psycho-synthesis, humanistic psychology, est, Arica Training, Transcendental Meditation, psychic healing, bio-feedback, mind control training, and yoga. (Donald Stone 1976) Most of the Holakuna Mystery

School participants had been involved with one of more of these disciplines. From the 1960s to the 1980s emphasis on spiritual aspects and practices increased within the human potential movement. (Meredith B. McGuire and Debra J. Kantor 1987; Roy Wallis 1985)

While the Holakuna Mystery School certainly did impart ancient secret techniques from Egypt and Hawaii, it was also firmly rooted in the human potential movement, both through "borrowing" from human potential disciplines and because many of its participants actively sought to expand their human possibilities. (Houston 1987) The extensive eclectic borrowing described above also typified the new age movement. (Stone 1976; Joan B.Townsend 2004.)

The human potential movement of the1960s was a progenitor of what in the late 1980s was called "the new age". In this book the term new age refers to a loosely connected movement of individuals and groups who adhered to one or more of the following precepts:

1. The course of history would radically change by the year 2012.
2. Humankind was about to make an evolutionary transition as a species becoming "higher" and better able to communicate with living things.
3. Human beings are capable of living together in harmony, fulfilling all their needs peacefully.
4. It is evident that humankind's psychic and spiritual abilities steadily increased in the last half of the twentieth century.
5. Help for making the above transitions is available from

extraterrestrials and spirits.

6. The natural environment will be recognized as humankind's foremost natural resource.

7. In ancient times human communities had reached technical and scientific levels equivalent to those of the twentieth century, but lost that knowledge through some cataclysm. (See Jeffrey L. MacDonald 1995 and Joan B. Townsend 2004.)

While an outsider would certainly have considered Holakuna Mystery School participants to be new age adherents, the participants themselves were reluctant to be closely associated with the movement, although each entertained at least some of the above precepts. There were frequent complaints about "new age fundamentalists' and "new age fascists" who were seen as being full of rhetoric about enlightenment, but behaving according to old learned patterns that would not facilitate spiritual regeneration. Elana lectured about the discrepancies in new age philosophy several times. No Huna group is mentioned in any of three new age directories I found in print in 1989.

Setting

During November 1987 through March 1989 the Holakuna Mystery School met at four different small conference centers on the West Coast for ten designated weekends. Two of these centers were on forested mountains. One was at the seacoast and one in the desert. One of the mountain retreats, which I call Paloma, was used for most of the sessions. Participants stayed in cabins or rooms in conference buildings at Paloma. A few stayed with nearby friends or drove home at night. Occasionally some participants slept in their cars or on the carpet in the conference room. This conference room was the setting where most mystery school activities took place. The room was small for a group of about forty people, perhaps thirty-five or forty feet square.

Typically those arriving early on Friday for a weekend session could step into the conference building and find Helen, who was training to be a Holakuna teacher, behind a table in the hall making room assignments, arranging transportation to outlying cabins, and dispensing information. There was laughter and conversation in the halls, the conference room, and the sleeping rooms, where participants were "catching up" on each other's lives during the interim between sessions. Participants expressed joy at their return and trepidation at the coming weekend of lectures, practices, and initiations, which they knew would be rigorous. They joked about this, and expressed empathy or elation as required by the accounts of life events related by others. At times this pre-session climate approached hilarity.

Journal entry: On Friday afternoon before the fourth session was about to begin I was assigned to a room in the conference building at Paloma with four nurses. (This room accommodated six or seven people.) The nurses, who had arrived early, were making jokes about "Nancy good-nurse who always saves lives," and at the same time putting on an impromptu fashion show for each other. Maureen had a new outfit much admired by the roommates, a draped dress of natural fabric, which could be worn in several ways. Maureen demonstrated the different ways the dress could be worn, and there was laughter as other roommates strutted between bunks in favorite casual outfits they had brought, imitating the poses of fashion models. They showed each other their quartz crystals,[3] jewelry, semiprecious stones, and earrings. Exclamations over these were punctuated with jokes and laughter. One nurse had recently quit her job, a move that the others applauded. There were humorous but biting remarks about the job demands placed upon nurses versus their own expectations for patient care.

Before the session began (A session usually started on Friday at 7:00 pm, after a 5:30 supper.) Regena was in the conference room, putting up beautiful bed-sheet size hand-painted wall hangings depicting the ancient Egyptian neters whose principles were associated with the theme of that weekend. For instance, the fourth weekend session dealt with the opening of the heart. Hathor, the neter of unconditional love, was represented in the form of a great blue cow. Regena had painted these hangings herself, and they always elicited praise from participants.

As they arrived, participants came into the room, placed their paraphernalia against the wall, and put a cushion, campstool, notebook, or tape recorder in the spot where they wanted to sit. Elana required all participants to bring the following items to sessions and keep them in the conference room during meetings: a staff, a bed sheet which was later fashioned into a robe, a small square wooden box, preferably cedar, and a knife. During the second and third sessions participants also brought toy stuffed animals at Elana's request. Most also brought notebooks and tape recorders.

Regena also set up the altar at the front of the room. A table draped with carefully centered colored cloths served for this. Objects that went on the altar had all been carefully packed. They included: statuettes of neters, semiprecious stones, scorpions in glass paper weights, sacred bundles of incense, crystals, candles, feathers, bells, brass bowls, carved stone eggs, seashells, wands, snake skins, deer antlers, and bones. (Participants often put their own objects on the altar as well).

In front of the altar sat a platform about eighteen inches high and covered with blankets, cushions, and what looked like a deer pelt. On this Elana sat during sessions. A seven foot tiered post or pillar constructed of cedar stood to the left of the altar. To the right there was usually an easel for charts, a blackboard, or a small bar-like counter. The room was carpeted, sunny, well lighted and ventilated. It opened on a porch in back proffering a view of the land below the mountains.

Directly across the hall from the conference room an open kitchen stood. There, lunch (in the form of vegetarian snack foods) was often served, and hot water and various teas were available. The rest of the conference building contained guest rooms, showers, bathrooms, and staff quarters.

Most meals, vegetarian in character, were served cafeteria style in another building. Meals were served at odd hours. For example on Saturday during the September 1988 session, breakfast was at ten

O'clock, snack lunch at one, and dinner at five, but on Sunday breakfast was at eight-thirty and lunch at twelve-thirty.

Notes

1. Whether Huna is indeed an ancient secret discipline is questionable. (See En.wikapedia.org/wiki/Huna_(new_thought) and also *The Sacred Power of Huna* by Rima A. Morrell,

2. See Chapter 5 for an account of events leading to Sally's withdrawal.

3. Holakunas, new age spiritual practitioners, and shamans may use quartz crystals for directing, magnifying, and storing subtle energy, as well as for boosting extrasensory perception. At mystery school Elana taught that a shaman may imprint a particular quartz crystal with all her esoteric knowledge and then hide the crystal or give it to someone for safe keeping so that she may find the crystal again after having died and reincarnated. Elana also taught that jewels are the compressed essence of qualities, the centers from which certain qualities enter the physical plane.

Chapter 2 Holakuna Knowledge

Sociologists call groups of people who depict the world and its processes quite differently from the rest of their culture, "cognitive minorities". Such groups often grow around ideas that deviate from accepted societal beliefs. (Peter Berger 1969). Those who chose to attend Elana's preliminary Holakuna classes and her mystery school elected to embrace such deviant knowledge. Since the adjective "deviant" carries a negative connotation, I prefer "alternative reality", a more neutral term.[1] Nevertheless, the mystery school reality appears to deviate sharply from the dominant worldview in the U. S. during the 1980s. Recordings of dialogue at mystery school lectures reveal participants eagerly seeking esoteric knowledge and collaborating with Elana in the elaboration of an ontology quite different from the one they had internalized during their lifelong acquisition of Western culture.

Basic Concepts

Basic Holakuna precepts most participants had acquired before

28

mystery school comprised a "deviant" view of the nature of the universe, humankind, power, and intention. Beginning students learned to direct subtle energy (spiritual energy or life force) by moving it through their bodies and out in streams for healing and manifesting. Subtle energy is considered to be a basic form of energy akin to electromagnetics but harder to detect, synonymous with life energy. It emanates from the stars, the sun, and the earth. Holakunas have an Egyptian name for it. This would appear to be the same energy Tanice G. Foltz described in her study of the Healing Hands Kahuna group. They called it Ki, characterizing Ki as an inexhaustible source of energy accessible through certain ritual methods, controlled and directed (usually through the hands) for healing (1985).

A specific technique for manifesting was taught in the preliminary Holakuna classes. By manifesting, practitioners brought a desired event, circumstance, or object into their lives. Usually what was manifested arrived in an ordinary way. Ruth, the oldest participant in the mystery school, told me about manifesting a nutritional product she needed:

> I use Barley Green and I'd run out of it. I hadn't been able to find a source for it. [Ruth was visiting in Oregon at the time of the interview and was cut off from her normal supplier.] I said to my friend Sally here in Oregon last week, "Sally, God, I'd give anything for the Barley Green I've been getting. I've got to get some." We drove up to a grocery store, a supermarket, and right alongside was this suburban (van) and it said "Barley Green." The

driver was a representative for Barley Green.

As one Holakuna teacher wrote in a letter to her students, "Even beginning students manifest well." Manifesting techniques combined breathing, mantras, meditation and visualization. Visualization is the Holakuna term for mental experiences during a trance state. Actually these experiences involve all the senses, not just vision. Imagery may be a more accurate term than visualization. (Allan Pavio 1986)

Life Style

Holakunas believe that everyone should be able to live with affluence in the life style they choose and that needy people have not learned how to direct their thought and emotion to manifest their needs and wants. There are no strict prohibitions on life style in Elana's teachings. Mystery school participants were advised to eat a macrobiotic diet, eliminating meat, nightshades (potatoes, tomatoes, peppers), and dairy products. Elana suggested that they give up drinking alcohol and smoking. At the second weekend everyone was given a pamphlet published by Eden Foods, Inc., of Clinton, Michigan, which offered guidelines for fundamental considerations regarding the Macrobiotic diet and way of life. This publication advised a diet consisting of 50-60% whole cereal grains, 5% miso or tamari broth vegetable soups, 25-30% vegetables (cabbage, Swiss chard, watercress, bok choy, escarole, dandelion, mustard greens, daikon, turnips, carrots, and certain squashes) and 20 % beans and sea vegetables (edible seaweed). Meat, eggs, animal fat, dairy products, tropical fruits, coffee, tea, aromatic herb teas, sugars, spices, and preservatives were to be avoided. Nevertheless there was no attempt to enforce the suggested diet either socially or through sanctions. Many mystery school participants continued to eat and drink as they pleased, and no one hinted they should reconsider.

Holakunas also embrace the concept of compassion, trying to accept and love everyone as they are. They seek to practice non-judgment, striving to never view other persons or themselves as bad or wrong. Elana advised her students to stand back, observe their interaction with another, and consider its possible consequences rather than condemn the action.

Nature of Life and the World

Beginning Holakunas learned of five elements, earth, water, fire, air and akasha, which is the element that dissolves all and contains all. Therefore akasha contains all knowledge. It represents a state preceding or underlying matter and energy. Practitioners use it for becoming invisible or making something invisible, and for dissolving blockages. The five are elements in the sense that a Westerner might think of states of matter. Each represented a physical force in the universe and had other associations. Seven directions are associated with certain principles, spiritual qualities, elements and colors. An extensive body of knowledge also surrounds thsee directions: South, West, North, East, above, below, and center.

Principles active in the universe personified and called neters interrelated closely with elements and directions. Although Elana

Learning the Mysteries

frequently represented them in the form of ancient Egyptian gods, neters were not just gods. Particular neters or gods may be referred to as

Table 2.1 Correspondences of Holakuna Elements, Faculties, Chakras, and Colors to Directions

North	South	East	West	Up/down
Air	earth	fire	water	Akasha
Mind	body	spirit	emotion	
Fifth	first	third	second	sixth
White	yellow	red	black	purple

archetypical figures, yet Holakuna neters signified more than their associated archetypes or some Euro-American characterization of pre-Christian gods and goddesses. For example, as neters the ancient Egyptian god Thoth personifies thought, a principle active in the world while Nut represents the sky and Geb, the earth: the two linked forever. Hathor represents love and compassion. (Geraldine Pinch 1994)

Recognizing that what westerners would call essences, forces, or principles (i.e. sky, thought, love) as neters (i.e. Nut, Thoth, Hathor) can take up personalities gives Holakunas greater influence over these principles. They can propitiate, channel, negotiate with, and even control neters. The following exchange took place at the second mystery school weekend:

> Participant: We need to change the archetypes. They are not frozen and fixed. We can change the archetypes and change all of us.

> Elana: Exactly! That's how we talk to the gods in this class. We're not only going to create a round table around which the gods can talk to each other, but we're also going to have to inform them of what we want their actions to be, because they were designed to be flexible. They were designed to go into the future.

The Physical and Spiritual Nature of Entities

Elana organized the mystery school curriculum around teachings about the chakras. The seven chakras are depicted as whirling disks or vortexes of subtle energy within the human body that are said to correspond to major nerve plexuses along the spinal column (B.K.S. Iyengar 1976; C.W. Leadbeater 1980; Swami Vishnudevananda 1960) Devotees of Eastern religions and various occult or spiritual disciplines in Western society are familiar with this concept.

In preliminary Holakuna classes students learned to locate, clear, and regulate the chakras in themselves and their clients. At mystery school participants learned that the chakras are actually seven different minds, each with its own teaching and separate point of view. Together with energy channels running through the body and minor vortexes in joints and extremities the chakras make up an energy body that interpenetrates the physical body. Each chakra is associated with a specific element and a neter or neters. The weekends of mystery school consisted of progressively opening and passing through these seven mind centers, plus much more. For some chakras more than one weekend was required to complete the associated teaching and initiations, hence the ten weekends of mystery school.

Holakunas hold a particular view of self, different from the usual Western view and related to the concept of chakras. They recognize a three-part division of the self, common to humans: the high self, low self, and middle self. The three selves are interdependent, and no one of them is thought to be more important or desirable than another. The high self is the God self, approximating a Christ within, or guardian angel. It has access to the most powerful, eternal realms of spirit.

In no way is the high self equivalent to Freud's superego. In Holakuna thought the superego or conscience is a function of the low self. The low self provides the functions of both superego and id. The high self accomplishes manifestation, divination, and promotes divine purposes in the mundane world. The low self includes or one might say unites the unconscious, the physical body and the autonomic nervous system. It encompasses emotional and body knowledge. The middle self resembles the conscious ego as Westerners know it, the logical mind plus the persona, the image a person projects in his social world.

The chakras, or separate minds, are distributed across these three divisions. The first two roughly comprise the low self, the second three the middle self, and the top two the high self. There is no direct communication between the high and middle selves. The high self can only be approached through the low self, and only when the low self is satisfied that all is proceeding normally, in the manner of a child that will cooperate with adults only when it feels secure. Hence, to function fully in and out of conscious social worlds, the individual must enlist the harmonious interaction of all three divisions of self.

Those ten weekends of mystery school constituted a journey comprising the opening of the seven chakras and their domains of knowledge and a successive honing and balancing of the three selves culminating in the completion of the high self body and resulting spiritual, emotional, social, and material advancement in the individual's life. However, such advancement takes much longer than the duration of mystery school, unfolding over many years. During each weekend the participants were led and eagerly plunged deeper into the Holakuna "deviant" reality.

Elana's Teaching Procedures

During the first four mystery school sessions most of the time was taken up with lectures. At Paloma, participants sat on the carpeted floor of the conference room in semicircular rows with a few seated on chairs around the walls. Elana sat in front on a platform raised about two feet above the floor and lectured. Lectures lasted for hours and they were complex. She used ancient Egyptian and Hawaiian terms and technical language drawn from psychology, medicine, physics, and esoteric literature, moving from one idea to another abruptly, leaving her students

Figure 5.1 The Chakra Minds and the Three Selves

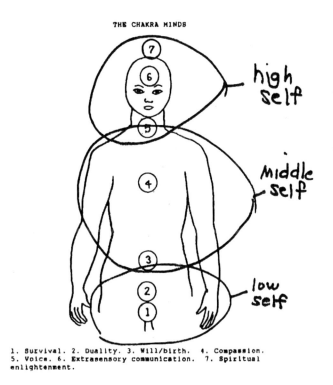

THE CHAKRA MINDS

1. Survival. 2. Duality. 3. Will/birth. 4. Compassion.
5. Voice. 6. Extrasensory communication. 7. Spiritual
enlightenment.

grsping for understanding. Yet during any given lecture we sat for hours, straining forward in rapt attention. (Lectures were punctuated with body movements and breathing exercises.) There was little fidgeting and seldom did anybody leave the room except at designated breaks. Question periods tended to be chaotic, with many questions asked and frequent interruptions, especially during the first weekends.

Initiation, empowerment, and ritual were important mystery school teaching processes. Long involved initiations were performed each weekend, with participants in an altered state of consciousness induced by Elana's voice and presence as well as the setting itself. These initiations involved visualizations, guided by Elana, in which participants experienced bizarre adventures, interacting with neters, elements, and directions. Initiations opened the chakras or energy channels and other spiritual or energetic body organs through psychic surgery. Guided visualizations involve a process, adventure or journey which the leader provides verbally usually accompanied with music and/or other sounds, invoking sensory images.[2] Each participant experienced these in her own way. (McGuire 1988; Gary Easthope 1985.) Holakuna psychic surgery involves using subtle energy to open or penetrate the energy body and change conditions there.

Whereas visualizing was done by the whole group together, Elana did the psychic surgery individually for each participant while all sat in trance. This procedure lengthened initiations by hours. Initiation sometimes involved ritual ceremonies such as candle burning, sacred meals, tying silk or cotton cords around the neck, and gifting of participants with ritual objects such as stones, shells, beads, or herbal mixtures.

Free style dancing, through which participants expressed their initiatory experience, usually followed initiations. For the dance a meditation music tape sufficed, or participant musicians provided music with violin, drum, and rattles, sometimes accompanied by group chanting of appropriate mantras.[2] Finally, empowerments were a type of initiation or an adjunct to initiation in which Elana imparted to participants the power to perform certain feats using subtle energy.

In addition to lecture and initiation, time was spent learning and employing practices and sharing individual concerns and experiences. For sharing, the group formed a circle. Each individual revealed his or her feelings, then received healing or feedback from the others. Specific practices furthered manifesting, healing self or others, and developing spiritual and psychic powers. Practices involved combinations of the following activities: chanting mantras, meditating, breathing, circulating subtle energy, moving the body, lucid dreaming, drawing symbols, and performing rituals (for instance a holakuna might burn a candle dedicated for a specified purpose). At mystery school practices could be done singly, in pairs, or with the group.

Elana employed a spiral curriculum. At each session many of the same principles were presented over again with a few new concepts added. Her use of the spiral curriculum was innovative. Each weekend the teachings were reintroduced from the point of view of the chakra mind explored that weekend; thus, participants didn't consider the teaching repetitive. This strategy seemed to bring about a deep level of learning in participants (Chapter 8), given that they were in an altered state of consciousness during teaching.

Elana prepared notes for her lectures but often disregarded them. She said she was channeling much of the material she taught, just letting the neters or her high self speak through her lips. The language she used during teaching was unusual. It seemed stilted, antiquated. An example follows:

> The will being formed in a very strong way, then is able to return to the second chakra, which is the heroic journey of Amon-Ra. What Amon-Ra does is that he is the neter of the return to that which was before chaos. The second chakra represents that which was the primordial deep before the coming of the light, the primordial deep wherein opposites are contained.

Much participant confusion resulted when middle class professionals used to business or academic speakers needed to adjust to Elana's use of symbolism and metaphor as a mode of learning and knowing. While at times she discussed scientific research and theory in logical, reasonable terms, most often her lectures employed metaphorical images. (See Susan Greenwood: 2009)

During regular conversation Elana did not speak in the manner she employed for lectures. Felicitas Goodman (1988) found that people in possession trance often speak with a particular lilt in their voice. During Elana's lectures and initiations such a lilt was noticeable especially when she used complicated, metaphorical language such as that quoted above. She seemed to exemplify possession trance speech as described by Goodman.

As a full participant observer during mystery school sessions, state of consciousness presented a huge problem for me. Sessions usually began with a visualization or practice, which would be done with participants experiencing an altered state of consciousness, a phenomenon recognized in anthropological research. Altered states of consciousness or changed perceptual states include: daydreaming, REM (rapid eye movement) sleep, and lucid dreaming, meditative states, hypnosis, and religious trance (Goodman 1988; Winkleman 2000). Altered states continued throughout the weekends. As one informant, Rudolph (a computer program designer who had been in "metaphysical work for over twenty years") explained, "I walk in and within five minutes I'm in an altered state. I pretty much stay that way for the whole weekend."

Elana's voice had a soothing, mesmerizing quality. Her lectures were difficult to understand. She used an array of scientific, literary, and ancient terms, and had a tendency to shift abruptly from one idea to another, leaving her students to figure out the relationship between the ideas. (I found that a relationship was always conceivable, but not obvious.) For all these reasons, during lectures participant attention was riveted on Elana.

At area group meetings between sessions, some participants complained that none of them had complete lecture notes. At times group members struggled to reconstruct what had been said during the previous mystery school session, checking their notes, recordings, official transcripts, and recollections in an effort to patch together some sequence. Occasionally there were gaps for which no one could remember what had happened.

Problems for Observation

After permission was granted for participant observation to begin (at the end of the fourth session), I discovered quickly that such observations were very difficult to do even during lectures. Each time I began an observation, I became enthralled by what Elana was teaching. The concepts were new to me. The terms were in an alien language, and my full attention was drawn from participants to the teacher again and again. My attention was already diffused by the altered state of consciousness we all were experiencing. There was no way to rely fully on tape recording. Since my recorder did not pick up voices from distant corners of the room, and neither did the official audio recordings, I frequently could not determine who had made a particular statement or what someone had said.

Gradually I learned during sessions to identify sequences of dialogue when they began, turn on the recorder, and hold it toward each speaker noting the day and time of the interaction, as well as each speaker's name, and as much of the content as I could write down. (My participant observation material up until participants granted permission comes from only recordings and my personal journal.)

An additional problem occurred when participants carried on a dialogue with Elana, dropped it when Elana resumed lecturing, and then picked up the same dialogue at a different time. In such instances I had to be able to identify the resumption of that particular thread of dialogue and return to my dialogue recording mode quickly, marking the place in my notes. Otherwise part of the interaction would be lost. This should have been easy, but given the state of awareness participants commonly experienced during lectures, it was not.

The First Weekend: Exorcism, Death, Quasi Resurrection

For the first weekend in November of 1987 I left Eugene, Oregon early Friday morning and drove to Paloma, a full day's drive. When I arrived, the session was already in progress. About 43 people were sitting on a floor cluttered with cushions and paraphernalia. Elana was sitting on her platform before the altar. To her left, leaning against the wall, was a full sized cedar coffin. (I had no doubt that I would be getting into it at some point that weekend.) To the right was the seven-foot cedar pillar hereafter called the post. I was asked to shut the door because a five-foot female python was crawling around the room. This was appropriate because the subtle energies holakunas work with are metaphorically depicted as snakes whose undulating movement represents waveforms. During the session participants patted and caressed the python.

A sharing was in progress. Each person was telling about themselves and what had occurred for them in the meditation and dream practice Elana had assigned in a letter to participants. Many people had experienced difficulties in their lives during the previous weeks. These included: problems with people at work, illness, and marriage and family conflict. Several participants reported that the money for mystery school tuition came to them unexpectedly.

Death

The participants had been told they would have to die. That first weekend included one death visualization on Friday night, a full death initiation on Saturday, and another initiation which opened certain chakras to better receive subtle energy, and a resurrection of the "emotional body." (Holakunas recognize at least ten different subtle bodies per person, each designated by its own Egyptian term. The emotional body and high self body are two of these.) This all meant that the initiates would be exploring the underworld, synonymous with the unconscious, the low self, which survives after death and is black.

One young woman, Annette, said that she was interested in what Elana had said about the dark unknown side of life, relating that she had much darkness in her, stemming from past lives, and she was bothered by it a lot, especially at that time of year.

Exorcism

Journal entry: November 10, 1987. On Saturday morning while Elana was lecturing, Annette said she was experiencing a lot of pain. She felt she was being split open down her front and her liver was being torn out. Elana called her up to the front of the room, had her lie down on the floor, and passed her hands over Annette's body several inches above it. She appeared to be using a technique in which the holakuna "sees" or "feels" what is amiss in the client's body through the hands while stroking the aura, the field of subtle energy surrounding a living body.[3]

Annette began to groan and thrash on the floor. She arched her back, her face reddened, and she threw her head back screaming and flailing her arms. Elana began to chant the Egyptian names of the seven medicine animals, who are helpers in the underworld, about which she had just been teaching, and signaled the participants to take up the chant. As 43 people chanted the seven ancient names over, one male participant, who was also a drummer, began to drum on a large (about 2.5' in diameter) handmade wooden drum with a leather drumhead. The participant violinist took up his instrument in accompaniment. Several women shook gourd rattles in rhythm, and one woman who looked to be near forty, with long gray hair and a pleasant face, shook her rattle around Annette's writhing body. This was Shoshona, a participant who was also a practicing Shaman.

Elana invoked each of the seven medicine animals by name. Each time she did this she ended by calling out something that sounded like "scummy," holding the "s" in a hiss and began invoking the next animal.[4] Annette quieted somewhat but continued to groan, choke, and

44

cry. Finally the exorcism was over. Annette lay sobbing on the floor, apparently no longer in pain. Later she was very quiet, and sat in the back of the room, answering in clipped sentences queries as to her wellbeing. At times during the day other participants held Annette in their arms or sat with her. By the next morning she was radiantly smiling, seeming completely relieved of her darkness. Between the second and third weekends Annette sent a letter to all participants stating that Elana's ministrations had helped her. In it she said:

> I want to speak to the powerful effectiveness of the exorcism performed by Elana on me in our first class. The experience opened and deepened me to the intense healing powers of the seven medicine helpers and I continue to work with them in exercising *kas.*

Initiation by Death

Much of the teaching on Saturday centered around death and the reenactment of death through initiation and visualization. Elana told us, "The practice that we are going to do is incredibly powerful because it approximates as closely as I know what begins to happen with death"

Later the following exchange took place, which indicated participants' trepidation about these experiences.

> Elana: We're going to stay in our [emotional] body for a while. How many of you noticed the difference?
>
> [Participanat laughter. Many raise hands.]

[Kim asked when the group would come back from their emotional bodies to their usual state. Kim was an attractive woman of 40 who was a personnel executive at a high tech corporation.]

Elana: No, you never come back. That's what I tell you.

Kim: I just wanted to make sure.

[nervous laughter from the group]

Elana taught that a holakuna must die with each breath and live in the moment.

Elana: The opportunity to die is [takes breath] here. That split second at the in-breath when it turns – voidness. Everything goes out of existence like a pendulum with every beat of the heart because the heart is going to bring the spiritual into the physical. It is the place with breath, heart, where we have the opportunity to influence the entire organism.

Carla: So we have to choose every second. [Carla was a woman in her thirties suffering from a debilitating physical condition. She walked with difficulty, leaning on a cane.]

Elana: Yes.

Carla: To do it again.

Elana: Yes.

Group laughter]

> Shoshona: I think that's probably the reason that the strobe lights in light shows in the sixties were so fantastic and terrifying. All they were saying – breath.
>
> Elana: Well said, Shoshona.
>
> Paticipant: yes because they showed us the truth and this was the way that the universe really is.

In this dialogue Elana suggests that participants can feel the difference in their bodies after initiation, and they do. Shoshona's and other participants' comments clearly support and reinforce Elana's version of what is. They are collaborating with Elana in the construction of this alternative reality.

A number of participants experienced headaches the first weekend. Elana explained and administered healing.

> Elana: And you have a headache too? You know I'm not surprised. These practices are very, very intense. As your consciousness alters, your body is interpreting what's happening to you as pain. If you could kind of think of it in those anomalous terms [sic.] -- Do you feel like taking in something that's mental right now?
>
> Headache sufferer: Yes, now.
>
> Elana: OK. [Claps her hands sharply.]
>
> Unidentified participant: Headache goes. Jeez, can we move?

Elana responded to this request for movement by teaching a Masai[5] dance which invoked the seven directions, using pre-Egyptian words.

Aka

The group performed the dance, and Elana went on to talk about *aka*, which is a subtle fiber that issues from human senses and from the chakras, and forms the basis for subliminal communication. She said that aka is a wave form. It is Brownian movement.[6] Aka forms nets of communication.

> Christy: I had an experience where someone was stalking me. I felt it but didn't see them until right at the last minute I turned around and they were there. I felt all this power rise up and come out my eyes, and they [the stalker] flew back about ten feet. While they were on the ground I ran and got away. Is that aka?
>
> Elana: Yes, that's aka. The net emerges from various points you have in your hands.
>
> Christy: I thought that it would be solar plexus, but I felt it go out my eyes.
>
> Elana: No, let me say that everything is aka. Everything has vibration. Everything has movement. Everything has intention, an intention, an intelligence, emotion, and sensibility. Everything is made up of that.

Elana also taught of descending *centropic* energies from the stars, that enter the body and of ascending entropic energies that rise up from the body. These are the energies holakunas work with, that emerge from points in the body as aka.

Building a New Reality

People came to mystery school with some knowledge of Holakuna beliefs from preliminary classes. Elana continued to build the deviant reality, giving everyday events like headaches new important meaning. (The incidence of headaches and nausea continued to be high.) Participants willingly collaborated with Elana in constructing the reality she presented, supplying examples and remembering cases from their lives that supported her premises. (This same process can be observed in elementary school classrooms.) Participants were frequently confused by what she was saying. In trance states during initiations and practices, they entered into and interacted in alternate universes that Elana created for them. This was undoubtedly an important facet of the construction of the alternative reality about which I could write little in detail, since my agreement with Elana prevented me from revealing the content of initiations and practices.

Notes

1. James A. Beckford (1985) decried sociologists' notion of deviance in his description of new religious movements (NRMs), arguing that NRMs have been characterized by social scientists as deviant and investigated through searching for factors which could account for that deviance. Beckfort complains that NRMs were being seized upon to illustrate themes and theories of social deviance and/or pathology, obscuring the importance of the NRMs in themselves.

2. Most of these tapes would be considered "space music" of the type played on the radio program "Hearts of Space" aired weekly on National Public Radio stations in the 1980s.

3. The aura is often perceived by psychics as a corona of colored light around the body. Holakunas describe it as an energy field surrounding and permeating the body. Tanice G. Foltz describes Kahuna "scanning," as a form of diagnosis in which subtle energy extensions are sent into the client. The "scanning" Kahuna might lightly run their hands over the client's body not quite touching it (1985).

4. This account of the exorcism, as Elana called the procedure, is taken from my journal and reflects how the events appeared to me at the time. This is not a formula for doing an exorcism. Later Elana explained the process involved. I didn't understand it at the time. (See Ralph B. Allison 1999.)

5. The Massai are a cattle herding people in Kenya. See Melissa Llewlyn-Davies (1981).

6. According to *Webster's Ninth New Collegiate Dictionary* Brownian movement is a random movement of microscopic particles suspended in liquids or gasses resulting from the impact of molecules on the fluid surrounding the particles.

Chapter 3 The Low Self

The second chakra mind has domain over dichotomy and polarity, gender roles and sexual energy. Much of the second weekend centered on participants' efforts to transcend social learning and childhood experiences surrounding gender roles. There was more contention among participants during this second chakra weekend than at any other session, as will be discussed below.

The Second Weekend: Water and the Second Chakra

This session was held in December of 1987 at a conference center even more remote than Paloma, a camp in a forest of small redwoods. There was a main lodge containing a conference room, plus a smaller room with a fireplace. Meals were served in a separate dining hall; participants were quartered in cabins. It was around 10:00 p.m. when I stepped into the conference room on Friday night. The participants were sitting on the floor in a circle and passing Elana's shaman staff from person to person. They called it the coyote staff because it was topped with a coyote skull, as well as being decorated with feathers, beads, and cords. Whoever held the staff had to tell what he or she least wanted the others to know and had to tell the truth. At times this process was suspended for a few moments in order to give support, counseling, healing, or hugs to the tearful truth teller.

During that weekend Elana opened participants' second chakras through initiation and taught about the element water in relationship to the second chakra. We learned about the symbol for water, which also represents birth and rebirth. Elana taught a song in ancient Egyptian, which celebrates the conception of the high self body in the second chakra womb. (Both men and women have this spiritual womb.).

Journal entry: December 13, 1987. For some reason I was particularly enthralled by the water symbol and second chakra song. They seemed very familiar like a favorite old toy from childhood. Since I had never heard the song or seen the symbol in that form before, I had no explanation for this feeling. (None of the other Holakuna symbols or chants affected me that way before or since.)

Duality

Elana presented her version of gender conceptions in prehistoric times as revealed to her by analysis of myth, new age literature on prehistory[1], and the Holakuna teachings she received from her benefactors. According to Elana, the adoption of a single male deity (without a model for divine femininity) resulted in the elevation of the god of war. Separation became valued above bonding, nature, and being a part of the whole. This is the view of the second chakra mind, which describes the world in terms of polarization and separateness. Elana said that Western culture and most of humanity operate from the second chakra as a base. Although some traditions emphasize using higher minds, and every person is capable of doing so, humanity still returns to the base of the second chakra. Separation, duality, polarization, and "making wrong"[2] underlie current human institutions.

As soon as mankind experienced the duality and struggle of opposites of the second chakra mind as the basis for interaction, one of the pairs of separate, distinct categories appeared more desirable than the other (good, bad; high, low; light, dark; male, female). This resulted in ranking everything in the world, making some qualities right, others wrong. People began to conceive of hierarchies, resulting in the subjugation of women and of feminine qualities in men. Elana gave examples from myth. She said:

> The great goddess of the Aztecs became the filth eater that wentfrom being the center of the universe to being the sacrificial knife   that demanded the heart be carved out. She was slain by her son   who sprang from her womb and slew her. Athena sprang from the   head of Zeus. The great power of the Universe became the great wife, until all across the planet we had the goddesses who are the   contemporary goddesses. Their power is the power of sexuality, the power of reproduction. We become the yin and yang, created   entirely by the male god. We have the womb of Vishnu, we have the   womb of Siva and of Rama. All of these are in search

of finding one's own power.

Having separated themselves from the feminine and dehumanized it, men had no access to the feminine power to give birth, so they had to steal women's power. Both hierarchy and "power over" were something a holakuna should be able to transcend. Participants performed chants and practices that took them back far into ancient times to heal their ancestors of past horrors. This was termed "re-membering" the past: a process of taking the past apart and putting it back together in a more advantageous way. In this case it was being done for ancestors. In one sense this meant visualizing changes in genetic material. In another it meant reinterpreting history. (Houston 1982.)

The initiations administered during the second weekend extended the possibility for initiates to go beyond the second chakra mind and establish a mental viewpoint of non-judgment, a perspective allowing bonding and oneness with humanity and the universe, rather than division and hierarchy. To accomplish this, both men and women had to reclaim the power that had been denied them by restrictive gender roles.

Contention

A great deal of controversy among mystery school participants accompanied these second weekend teachings. Stress was augmented by a windstorm and loss of electricity for most of Saturday and Sunday. On Saturday afternoon each person did a practice with a partner in which partners took turns assuming their high self. The high self answered questions for the other partner. At the very moment Elana guided the first partners to manifest their high self a strong gust of wind shook the building and all electrical power went out for a thirty-mile radius. (The immediate cause was reported to be a tree limb blown down severing power lines and damaging a transmitter.) The outage lasted about ten hours, during which there was no heat except the fireplace and only windows for light.

Some male participants (males were always in the minority at mystery school) seemed to respond to their perception that they were being blamed for the gender inequality Elana had described.

Participant: You're saying we never had a creation myth that was whole.

Elana: Yes.

Participant: Because of all this, of that masculine --

Elana: Right.

Participant: I wanted [to say] something important. There was a creation myth previous to that that did incorporate both the god and the goddess as one.

Elana: Well they did. That's what the myths are. . .

[later]

Paul : You're talking about love, sexual relationship and spiritual relationship that happen together, and there's an actual dependency. [Paul was a therapist, a man in his forties.]

Elana: Oh yes.

Paul: I'd like to argue against that. That it is possible to exceed that dependency.

Elana: Oh, I'm not saying that's not possible. I'm saying that the image, the models we've had in our gods have said it's not possible.

Paul: Yes I --

Elana: I'm saying that we have to inform the gods that this relationship is possible. What I'm saying is exactly what you're saying. . . .

Paul: I agree and I guess my feeling is that energy is being focused too much on the negative from the past in this workshop. I guess I feel very strongly about that and the need to be positive.

Elana: And healing. That's what we're working toward in the fourth session.

As people began to examine their past experiences surrounding gender roles, personal anguish surfaced.

Jill: For me to claim my power I need to say one thing to the group. [Jill was a woman in her early fifties, who worked with seriously ill and dying people.]

Elana: Come here [to the front]. Say it right now with the microphone.

Jill: Woe. Hear me. I want the group to hear this. It's not anything that we didn't already know but I need to say it aloud.

The Friday night when I was saying, "I hate my mother: I hate my mother." I want to really emphasize that for me the harm, the pain, the suffering that I've gotten from the masculine, what we're calling the masculine, whatever, has come in biggest share from people in women's bodies. I want that heard because I want some of you here in this room to know me, to know how badly I've been hurt by your masculine image. Thank you.

Processing

During lectures, practices, and initiations in the early mystery school weekends individuals would begin to sob, gag, cough, and sometimes vomit, requiring assistance, empathy, and personal healing from Elana and the others. Participants called this behavior "processing." There didn't seem to be any warning for the onslaught of "processing" and the participant anthropologist could not help wondering if she was going to be the next one crying, gagging, and rolling on the floor. Elana said that when one participant went through this they were doing it as a proxy for all the others. All would benefit.

An instance of processing, which also illustrates contention over presumed choice of what the group could do next, occurred on Sunday just before lunch.

Elana: How many of you don't want to talk about it? I asked you at the beginning, do you really want to work deep on [sex and gender issues] or do you want to not? There is a way of bringing them together. In the fourth session they come together. Here at the second chakra they polarize.

Virginia: Can we do something so we don't go into lunch? It's just about time for lunch and I'm just wondering about something to get our energy up to a better place. I don't want to listen to the conversations that are going to go on at lunch today. [Virginia was an educator in her forties.]

Elana: you don't want to?

Virginia: No, I don't.

[Chorus of voices].

Unidentified participant: You don't want to go to lunch? You might not have a choice.

[Laughter and talk]

Virginia: If you feel you need to do some griping it's important to talk about it. Don't read me wrong. I just want something, something of a resolution before we go to lunch.

[More laughter, babble]

Male voice: Resolve the whole session before lunch!

Female voice: I don't need a resolution.

Others: I feel great. I feel good.

Elana: That's what we're doing in the next process [meaning practice] . . .

Virginia: I want to do something before lunch.

[Loud, incredulous laughter. Participants spread their hands in a gesture of resignation.]

Virginia: If you want to stay, I'm really concerned about the energy level. Am I reading the energy level in this room wrong?

Some participants: No, No.

Female voice: I feel free,

Others: I feel great. I feel good.

Elana: I would like to do this process before lunch too, and lunch is now. That's the way it's called up.

Lisa: I think the amplification of the negative is important so that we can do the process later. [Lisa was a middle-aged woman who was a therapist, much respected by other participants. [Throughout mystery school Lisa often spoke as a mediator in support of Elana as she did here. Lisa frequently asked Elana to supply tactile or olfactory imagery during visualizations because she could not visualize.]

Elana: The amplification of the negative! You will never have the chance to reclaim your power unless you know what has been taken from you right this minute.

Virginia: I'm going to get into it. I'm just frustrated with the timing.

Elana: I know that the timing is not necessarily the way we would have it. Is there any way you can let that be ok?

Virginia: [Sobbing] No.

Elana and Virginia missed lunch while Elana helped Virginia heal anger over childhood negation power. The electricity came back on during lunch. They said it happened at the moment Virginia received her power.

It seemed that the participants' behavior throughout this weekend was childlike. The processing resembled temper tantrums. The arguments over procedure and gender history were in structure like those heard in a grade school classroom or on a playground. Was the whole group regressing to childhood?

Journal entry: January 29. 1988. A week before I went to the third session in January of 1998 I had an amusing dream. I dreamed that many participants had brought little pigs to mystery school. Pigs were running all around an already crowded conference room. A woman there told a story of how her mother used to raise pigs and loved to look at them, but after a while the mother got very tired of having pigs around and didn't want them ever again. When I awoke I couldn't figure out what the dream meant.

The Third Weekend: Amon-Ra and the High Will

I arrived back at Paloma late again on a Friday in January 1988 during a break just before the passing of the coyote staff. Months later Nancy, one of my informants, spoke of her experience with the coyote staff: (Nancy was a health care worker, and the youngest participant in mystery school.)

A feeling comes in me that I absolutely cannot be that part of myself
that cannot say what it is I'm feeling. . . . That stick, the coyote
stick, does the same thing to me. Anytime you're creating any kind
of ritual about telling the truth it's real for me. It's real hard not to
[tell the truth].

Journal entry: January 29, 1988. When the coyote stick came into my
hand that night I heard myself say that the thing I least wanted the group
to know was that I ate more than half the food in my household (of two)
and did less than half the housework. Then I realized that the dream of
pigs at mystery school touched on just this matter and that it was time to
work on my problem of "piggishness."

A cloth painted with a life sized figure of Amon-Ra hung suspended
behind the altar that weekend. Amon-Ra is the neter associated with the
third chakra mind of fire, will and sun, located in the solar plexus area.
Elana taught that there were two kinds of will, high and low. She said the
low will is actually where people experience the duality emanating from
the second chakra. (We had experienced it at the previous session.) The
high will is the place of centering and being in the moment. The high
will is actually situated in the second chakra, at the spot in the body
where the ascending (entopic) energies and descending (*centripic*)
energies merge forming the still point or *so*, which is the focus of
existence. The high will received more attention that weekend than the
actual third chakra. Elana performed three initiations involving long

visualizations to open the third chakra and mobilize the high will. A number of practices were taught.

Reprogramming

Elana instructed participants on how to reprogram khas. Khas, complexes or parts, are considered to be little entities. According to Elana they can range in nature from bad habits to demons. The low self (unconscious) is made up of khas, which were also referred to as "old tapes." Many of them are beneficial, but others outlive their usefulness, and inhibit self-development because they keep running an old detrimental program. (We could also look at khas as neural pathways.) A behavior that inhibits social interaction like extreme loudness in conversation, or an unhealthy habit like smoking is a kha. At one time these behaviors were useful to their owner, but after they cease to be useful, khas are hard to change.

Reprogrammed khas were always reincorporated back into the owner's unconscious, even if they were demons. (See Ralph B. Allison 1999) Elana exorcised khas from Annette the first weekend. She taught several techniques for dealing with old khas for either the holakuna or their patients, including exorcism. Participants commented on the obvious similarity between these practices and Bandler and Grinder's neuro-linguistic programming (1982). Neuro-Linguistic programming, however, did not use archetypes, archaic symbolism, and mantras, nor did it refer to spiritual body organs, all of which Elana's Holakuna practices did. Elana also taught participants how to build a new kha in order to institute a desired autonomic behavior, in this case Holakuna breathing for higher consciousness.

Journal Entry: January 29, 1988. On Sunday morning I rose early and stood for a few minutes on the deck of the conference room. Fog had just lifted and the sun was shining. As the sun warmed me I felt warmed by a great love, radiating through my body. I had never felt such a thing before. It was a moving, unexplainable, an entirely unexpected experience.

Multiple Realities and Breath

At breakfast there was discussion and some complaints regarding the way Elana asked the group to make choices about what to do next or when to have break. Some participants said everyone took too much time discussing the options without ever reaching a decision. There were complaints that the sessions were not well organized and we were wasting too much time during lectures with interruptions for questions or processing. (Initiations were never interrupted.) Some admitted that they did not understand what Elana was talking about much of the time.

On Sunday Elana lectured about a person's capability to align universes and the perception of multiple realities. She spoke of how people in some eras had universal agreement about such precepts as "fire burns." The agreement creates a universe in which certain things are possible and certain others are not, for instance fire walking. When you identify with a certain mind stream, she said, "That becomes the layer in which you will walk." The more agreement one gets from others (both agreement of individuals and agreement of the third eye and will) about what one perceives, the greater the likelihood of creating an entire universe into which one can step.

The technique of stepping into another universe is one means of Holakuna healing. Elana said that if one wanted to remove a tumor from a client, one did not have to dematerialize it. In the universe where the tumor was, one could create the thought that the client did not want that tumor. The healer could get the third eye, the high will and a lot of other mind streams (khas, people) all in agreement and then, becoming one with the patient, just align the two universes and step into the one with no tumor. This revelation brought a round of questions and explanation.

Lisa: You said the *so* is simultaneously coalescence and destruction. [The Holakuna concept here termed *so* is best described as the center of being in any entity. I have changed the Egyptian name for it here.]

Elana: Yes, yes. Coalescing and destruction . . . is the still point, the ush [the void] and the breath. That's why you don't have to worry about destroying something or taking it out. Everything is taken care of in that instance [The step into the aligned universe]. . . .at that point of simultaneity. . . .

Lisa: is that . . . the way the breath comes out?

Elana: This is the still point [indicating between the second and third chakras. She explained further.]

Male voice: Could you answer a question about—

Female voice: Getting into questions again!

Paulene: The wrapping of the breath around--? [Paulene was a health care professional who made gourd rattles with finely detailed designs. She impressed me as an outspoken, no-nonsense type of person.]

Elana: Yes, the breath around the still point. It's metaphoric in one sense because the example is everything that is.

Voice: o--k!

Elana: What we're doing is we're going to a very deep level and we can only use metaphors. What we have is the breath. The way that the breath functions does not lend itself to structural stability. It's like what Jackie was talking about. She said you have to use mechanics that allow for negative time in order to solve the puzzle but we're living in a world that doesn't allow for the mechanics of negative time to be introduced as a reality . . . and so the puzzle cannot be solved. [Laughter].

Elana: Does that make sense?

Voices: Yes.

Yes.

NO!

Ruth: We have it when we dream. . .[Ruth was seventy-four years old and had spent many years studying a yogic tradition which emphasized the power of sound.]

Elana: Thank you, Ruth. There's a wonderful example. Ok, you tell me how a dream is structured and I'll tell you –

[laughter].

Elana: . . . . So the closer you get to the still point, the closer you get to power, because it's not power over anyone. When we talk about power we just have to get beyond that word. It's like God. Say power and everyone goes to sleep.

Unidentified participant: Heh!

[Group laughs.]

Elana: And then we get engaged, right? So we want real power. Instead of taking forever for me to explain all this you just have an experience of it by doing the practice. . . . Now I'll take two or three questions and then the practice.

Shoshona: In your statement about the tumor, so one way that we can at least look at it in our heads is that the practitioner and the person through agreement and through breath are literally shifting that person into another universe where--.

Elana: You're literally walking in another universe.

Shoshona: Yes, where the tumor no longer exists.

Elana: Right. Then you don't have to change it. They don' t have to have created it. [Referring to the contention that new age adherents place responsibility for illness squarely on the sick individual][3]

Shoshona: No guilt, no blame, just this shift.

Elana: Just this – right – the problem I have with the [new age] community is this. There's this tumor, right? There is also mercury in the water stream. There is the aluminum cookware that was used, not knowing.[4] Then there are the manufacturers of that cookware, and there are all the people who allowed the standard to slip. In my town what they do is, when the mercury goes into the water they just up the amount that's safe to drink.

[Bitter participant laughter, ha, ha].

Elana: Now I'm with this because maybe this person drank a lot of coke or ate a lot of things with preservatives in them and then had a lot of thoughts about wanting to die, but had those thoughts . . . because their mother was beating them because her father raped her and her father raped her because his mother molested him because--Where does it end? Who created this tumor? Who did that? And then I say, "Well, I did it? All by myself!"

[General loud laughter]

Elana: Where is the "I" here? Walking between the worlds takes us out of that whole thing. There's no blame then.

Issues

Several issues that came up repeatedly at mystery school were expressed in the dialogue above. One was current popular concern in the West about environmental health hazards emanating from industrial production. Another was Elana's belief, shared with participants, that new age healers were missing the point when they said individuals generate their own disease through their thoughts and response to emotional traumas.

Although holakunas certainly think this is possible, Elana suggested here that sickness has multiple causes. Causality may be impossible to establish. She questioned Western notions of causality itself. Another dynamic in this exchange was participants' uncertainty as to whether they understood Elana. (I noticed that only a few of the forty-some were asking questions.) Elana reassured them that their logical mind did not have to understand:

> Elana: That's another thing. The initiations are meant to speak to this other mind that we're forming. Your logical mind is just along for the ride to remind you to do these practices . . . You are getting at a deep level of information that you just are not used to using. What I really want to emphasize is, if you're in confusion, it is actually the highest state you can be in, because usually what that means is you can't file anymore back in the same old box.
>
> Voice: Oh, good.

Although participants continued to complain about Elana's lack of organization and her use of time for individual processing, they demonstrated support for her at the closing circle that third weekend, insisting that she stand in the center to receive energy from the whole group. The Holakunas agreed to visualize the circle every day sometime between 8 a.m. and 12 noon with Elana and anyone else needing group support in the center. After the group took many minutes to decide on a time when they could all do this, Elana told them they needed to learn that all time was the same for their circle.

Notes

1. Elana frequently cited Riane Eisler's (1988) *The Chalice and the Blade: Our History, Our Future* and Sam Keen's (1988) *Faces of the Enemy: Reflections of the Hostile Imagination.*

2. Elana used the expression "making wrong" to mean vilifying or abasing the other person, viewpoint, behavior, etc. If something was made wrong, the opposite became right.

3. Meredith McGuire (1988) reports on various alternate healing adherents' beliefs about the causes of illness. For followers of traditional metaphysics the primary cause of illness in a person was their erroneous thinking. McGuire found that meditation and human potential groups listed pollution, imbalance, emotions, and stress, as causes of illness and some of them blamed the individual's ego. Psychic and occult healing groups blamed factors the individual can control such as thought patterns, habits, attitudes, values, and response to stress.

4. Many alternative healers and health 'purists" believed that aluminum cookware is toxic. Some cited the late Jethro Kloss (1975) who reported (quoting an article by Dr. Charles T. Betts) that the U. S. government in 1930 provided evidence for the assumption that aluminum pots are harmful in Federal Trade Commission Docket 540.

Chapter 4 Entering the Middle Self: the Holy Family

Journal entry: March 12, 1988. For the March 1988 session I arrived at Paloma early Friday afternoon. I helped Regena and Joe put up the wall hangings for this session. Behind the altar we hung Hathor, neter of the heart, compassion and birthing, in the form of a great blue cow. Khonsu, the neter of healing went on the left wall. We used masking tape because the Paloma staff had asked us not to put tacks in the wall. I helped carry in and unpack the objects that went on the altar and watched Regena set it up, and I was present for the nurses' playful "fashion show" (Chapter 1). This weekend the idea of my study was to be presented to the school for approval and I was anxious to hear what they would say about it.

The Fourth Weekend: Heart and Bonding

This was the weekend of the fourth chakra, which is called the heart center. The first evening after opening circle Elana summarized what would be covered in the ensuing two days:

We are at the edge of truth when we come to a place where we must handle paradox within us to contain it without resolution, without

70

judgment, and without retaining any thoughts whatsoever of regret, or hope. Such is the paradox of the heart. Focus now on your heart and make yourself ready to come home. Coming home means breaking through to the perfection that already exists, and to do so without trying, for it is a powerful principle that if you try when it is based on a belief that you are not all right and you are not perfect already, you will perpetuate and thereafter maintain that belief.

Bonding

Elana said the purpose of mystery school was to provide re-parenting, since if a baby is not comforted, nursed, and allowed to begin breathing naturally when born, it does not receive the stimulus necessary for completion of certain nerve circuitry in the reticular brain. If these circuits are not developed the whole system will continue trying to complete them for life. The un-bonded individual will keep trying to have these basic needs met rather than go on to develop new brain circuits.

Through resonance the un-bonded adult could be restored to a fullness of heart, making her capable of bonding with everything and everybody in the world. By resonance Elana meant Holakuna use of reverberation and harmonics in chanting mantras. In Elana's classes and at mystery school holakunas learned particular ways of making sounds instrumental for changing matter and events. They learned to produce harmonics when chanting. They learned certain utterances and notes which produced specific effects. Since vibration is the basis of everything, Holakuna chants could bring about changes in organisms at the cellular level and beyond. These mantras were said to be especially effective, because the words had been used by pre-dynastic and dynastic Egyptians for thousands of years. Participants generally agreed that the Huna mantras are powerful.

Julie, a thirty-nine year old "family and abuse" counselor, spoke of the healing practices known as toning in which the Holakuna utters two or three notes at the same time:

> I was with a friend, camping, and his back really hurt. I said, "Well, I just learned this. Let me try this [toning]." We were up high in the mountains, above the timberline in kind of a little *circ*. It was flat and sort of rounded so there was a possibility of some geological stuff going on in terms of the sound. I made the sound, actually I should say I let it come through, and for both of us the hair went up on the back of our necks, because the sound was like there was a group of people standing there. When that was over he was fine. His back didn't hurt.

Elana explained that the Holakuna initiations and practices would make participants fully bonded beings as they went through age regression in altered states accompanied by sound and breathing. This, Elana said, was more than just guided visualization. She noted that professionals called the un-bonded state attachment. Major religions taught that the needs of the un-bonded were wrong. Instead of satisfying the needs they offered varying notions of who the bad guy was, or followed the strategy of transformation. "You just go out and transform all the people who are 'wrong' and the world will be fine." One saw these ideas operating in the new age as well as in traditional religions. Elana said:

> There is a kind of new age fundamentalism setting, which is just a whole lot of new pat answers in exchange for old pat answers. This is the tendency of the un-bonded heart. It's not wrong. It's the un-bonded heart that has to be secure.

Elana had outlined one difference between Egyptian Huna and the major religions and new age belief systems: the response to the un-bonded heart. Rather than responding to that state, Holakuna would make its adherents bonded.

Illness and Suffering

On Saturday morning a great deal of time was taken up with discussing the welfare of Jackie, who had been seriously injured in an automobile accident on the way home from the third mystery school session. Participants wanted to know what they could do both on a spiritual and a mundane level to help Jackie. Those who had visited her, including Elana, reported on her condition. Marsha, who had driven the accident vehicle, received expressions of concern and support from the group.

Elana said her teacher, Marta, taught that people who are sick and suffering are actually carriers of messages from the future about what's working. They are masters who are providing an opportunity for others to learn. Elana spoke again of how the new age fundamentalists maintained that thought causes illness. Though illness might be called psychosomatic; mind, body, heart, soul, and emotion were all definitely involved in illness. That did not mean thought was the cause. Looking for causes was looking for pat answers. Pat answers prevented direct perception.

At the level of creation, Elana lectured, illness is synchronistic, not causal. She implied that human attention influences matter and energy. "The minutest particles of matter and energy are a vortex or vibration: a sound formation, a quality," she said. The minute an observer's attention is focused on a particle, its quality changes.[1] This focused attention amounts to a co-creation that influences the entire nature of the universe. Illness is an expression of spirit, but people's links with each other in the net of aka mean that there is no one sick person in a family. If one is sick, the whole family is sick. People are interpenetrating fields. With illness the whole field is disturbed.

A participant commented that her mother's death healed all of the family in different ways. "Yes," Elana replied, "It always has a purpose that is positive." She told the group that they must get out of mass consciousness. Rather than approach curing as war, as, for example, the "war on cancer," the Holakuna healer approaches the intelligence behind the disease and communicates with it. It was even possible to extend consciousness to communicate with one's own cells individually. (As Elana spoke these words I heard three tiny popping sounds issuing from one of the wall hangings.) "Emotion is physical," Elana lectured. "Pressing up against emotional scars is one of the ways healing begins." At this the Khonsu hanging launched itself from the conference room wall on my left in one graceful swoop. Participants laughed loudly, undoubtedly assuming this was a clear endorsement of Elana's words by the principle of healing.

On Saturday Elana guided the participants through a very long initiation, including the elements of regression, sound, and breathing. This initiation was too long to be given to the whole group in one sitting. The bulk of it was done on Saturday and the rest was divided into sectors administered between lectures and practices for the rest of the session. At the end of the first sector every participant received an Egyptian name from the mystery school teacher.

Gifting

Several participants were selling things during breaks at mystery school that weekend. Ann was selling silk scarves she had hand painted with Egyptian figures. Zelda was selling official tapes and transcripts of the second and third sessions. Others were selling their photographs of Elana, of the wall hangings, and of the altar plus various artifacts. Regena sold special quartz crystals for radionics boxes.[2] Elsa offered her inspirational greeting cards. Zelda, a tireless organizer, was instrumental in encouraging participants to make available goods they had access to which other holakunas might want. The participants had discovered it was difficult to find some things useful in the practice of Holakuna.

Certain herbs, oils, and magical supplies not commonly available had to be ordered from little known shops in distant cities.

On Sunday afternoon participants cleared the conference room floor of pillows, camp chairs, notebooks, recorders, boxes and staffs and sat in a circle. All had been told in a letter from Elana to bring a gift that symbolized the qualities that they had to give the world, from the direction they had sat in around the circle on the compass rose. The direction could be North (mind, air), East (spirit, fire), West (heart, water), South (body, earth), or center (akasha). One person at a time went to the center of the circle and told what directions they had sat at, and what qualities they needed in their life now.

Elana said, "Allow yourself to be pulled from your heart to the center. As you listen with great compassion to that person you will know if you have the gift which will answer that call."

Gifts ranged from expensive looking jewelry and treasured keepsakes to a bottle of spring water and a pot of earth. Everybody received an appropriate gift. Two examples of what I mean by appropriate follow. One woman asked for something from the West; she received a black stone with a natural white cross on it. She said she had been walking the beaches in the past weeks looking for her special stone. When it was her turn Ruth said she could not think of anything she needed. She already felt complete. Wilson, the drummer came up, saying he was the only person who did not bring a gift that weekend, so he gave Ruth nothing (except a big hug).

When all the gifts had been given one person was missed. As some were getting up, Nancy came into the center of the circle and said she knew that there was no gift for her. She offered her teddy bear for Jackie in the hospital. Later she told me:

> The day of the gift exchange, God, I was in that so much it was absolutely horrible, and then to get into the middle of the circle. I knew that I was the last one and there was no gift for me. It was typical of my family to not get what I needed. It was so typical to feel abandoned and to feel separated. Yet it had a different ending.

Elana had a gift for Nancy, a beautiful semi-precious stone bracelet.

Elana said that the point was, our needs would be provided for.

Nancy had told me more about her relationship with the mystery school:

> It's the ritual and the ceremony, the sacredness of that group, I think that makes me bond with them. They also really mirror my family in so many ways. That's really incredible because when I initially came to the group a lot of the time I would feel the way I did when I was a little kid around not belonging and not being taken seriously, and being the youngest, and that people didn't want to see me there and they didn't want to hear.

> Being in this group and having them mirror my family the way they do gives me a chance to recreate the stuff that caused me so much pain when I was a kid, but it also gives me the opportunity to give it a different ending and make it a healing instead of a wounding.

The tone of the interaction between participants and teacher the fourth sessions differed from the first three sessions. Participants continued to collaborate with Elana in building the alternate reality. They were still confused by her teaching, but they were now confused in solidarity. In some way the building of the holy family had been accomplished by the fourth weekend, just as Elana had said it would, when I asked her to let me do this study. Nancy had confirmed as much.

Journal Entry: March 20, 1988. Today I took a two-mile walk to the west of my apartment in the Willamette Valley, Oregon. I was worried because there hadn't been enough rain or snow in Oregon that winter. The breeze picked up and blew on my fingers and face as I walked. It blew between my fingers and made them tingle and vibrate. It was as if the wind were trying to communicate with me. I used the Holakuna practice for engaging the third eye for communication, but I forgot to use the mantra. The words came into my mind, "It's raining in the West." That was no surprise since the weather report predicted light rain on the coast.

March 23, 1988. Last night the first major Pacific storm in seven weeks blew into the Willamette Valley, bringing heavy rains. (It was hovering off the coast on March twentieth.) The night of March twentieth I dreamed I was lying in bed on my stomach and one cat was sitting upright and very alert on either side of my chest. The wind was blowing and it was singing "awh" in male voices at about middle C. A votive candle sat on either side of the bed in the dream and two spirits were teaching me, showing me a symbol that looked like a knot. I woke up. One cat was curled up on either side of me and a wind chime on the porch was sounding one note over and over again.

March 28, 1988. I had the same dream with the cats and the two teachers. This time they were teaching me about the three selves, and chanting in the same voices as before, "The *so* is the source. The *so* is the source," over and over. They showed me a chart outlining the human body. A golden spark indicated the position of the *so*. The spark moved from chakra to chakra on the chart. As the *so* moved, the low self and middle self also moved. The low self was a spot of brownish orange light, and the middle self was yellow.

Notes

1.According to Fritjof Capra particle physicists cannot honestly characterize themselves as objective observers since, through observing they influence the properties of the particles they study. (1984)

2.Radionics boxes were handmade receiver/transmitters for subtle energy.

Chapter 5: Bonding and Changing

The fifth and sixth Holakuna weekends concentrated on healing and balancing the middle self through the heart and throat chakras. While the fourth weekend at Paloma centered in bonding with the holy family, the fifth involved bonding with one's individual Egyptian neter. This was to be accomplished outdoors in a very unusual part of a Pacific Northwest desert.

The Fifth Weekend: The Throat Chakra

Mystery school was scheduled to meet in a very small town. There was no conference center per se, only a motel and the town hall for lecture sessions. At the last minute Elana and Larry discovered this building was not adequately heated. Town officials offered their high school choral room as a replacement. It was much like other rooms in which the mystery school had met. Instead of an altar Elana's helpers set up a table covered with rock crystals. The neter hanging on the front wall was hidden behind a plain sheet.

This session was to deal with the opening of the throat chakra mind that rules breath and voice, also called the high heart. We would deal with adult bonding, and bonding with the high self in the form of an aspect of a neter. Elana had determined the personal neter of each participant using their astrological charts[1] and meditation. This neter was called their beloved, personifying their high self. The beloved is the part that one feels is missing from one's life. All this seemed to have more to do with the high self than the middle self.

Elana explained:

The middle self comprises a combination of will [high and low will], the heart, and the second chakra just up to the heart. The high self is the high heart [throat] including the head. You have these three interacting principles. The middle self, which is our ordinary consciousness, even though it's evolving into a high self, can only evolve itself through the low self.

She said that mystery school was to awaken honesty by showing that our awful feelings associated with parental commands and edicts from childhood are a fiction. This could only be discovered by facing what's really in the low self. Participants had done this in the first three sessions.

Elana explained that khas are real because they are neural chemistry, actual formations of the brain (neural tracks) many of which result from our response to trauma. Like everything in the universe a kha begins with a vibration or sound, which is the human's expression of a feeling. The same sound goes out into the universe like a beacon and attracts like khas in the form of other people and events, so that the same unwanted experience keeps happening to a person over and over. People become the puppets of their experience.

She drew a model of time on the board, a circle with now (i.e., the present) in the center and different times represented by different points in the circle. The high self is in this circle time frame, perceiving everything happening at once, but the middle self usually perceives time as linear. Elana said we know when the high self is communicating with us because it gives us a coincidence, a synchronicity. Since the group had shared synchronicities and experiences of enlightenment and also initiations, they had bonded together in a family.

During an interview the day after the sixth session Elsa, a forty-two year old teacher who worked as an interim instructor, (taking different sorts of teaching jobs) told me:

We're here to bond with each other and that has been a big learning process. I went through a lot of alienation with some of the members. Finally, at this mystery school [session], I saw that we can totally accept each other. It doesn't mean we're going to be total best friends, but we can look at each person with love and really see who they are. That's a unique experience.

The Beloved

The journey through the chakras appeared to facilitate a process of human psychological development. Participants first bonded with the mystery school group as a family, and then with their neter. Elana said this bonding with family and with "the beloved" formed a matrix for the next step in the Holakuna quest, entering the void. If a person should enter the void un-bonded, when they hadn't found the beloved, they would enter united with the shadow, the dark unknown part of the low self (unconscious).

To this revelation participants responded: Oh," "Mmm," "Woof," and "Very heavy." Elana mentioned Hitler as someone who had entered the void bonded with the shadow.

Participants were each to be told the name of their beloved neter aspect at the end of the initiation on Saturday, but they would all use *Sekhmet*, the principle of enlightenment for bonding during the initiation (all the neters are one). Sekhmet and all beloved neters are both male and female, containing the paradox of the sexes. This enables them to meet every human need. When the covered wall hanging was unveiled, it turned out to be Sekhmet, the lion headed goddess, naked, with an erect penis and pendulous breasts. (As a former public school teacher it bothered me to see this figure hanging in the high school choral room.)

Some participants shared their perceptions and experiences regarding the high self. Ed who was a psychiatrist with what he called "a traditional practice," said an oversimplification would be "as above, so below. If you have this beautiful unity within, you're going to have it easier on the outside." Elana agreed. Vanessa, a fifty-five year old family therapist, who often encountered difficulty communicating her psychic and spiritual ideas in terms other participants could understand, spoke of her long intense experience of knowing the beloved, and of the opposite, the times when she did not have that knowledge in her life. She called this state of affairs paradox and polarization. Elana said that Vanessa was able to contain the paradox.

A third participant asked, "Someone like Mother Theresa who is constantly in a state of ecstasy, where is she containing? Is that the external containment of the Shadow that she's working with?"

Elana replied:

Yes, she's working with her external shadow. See, then it manifests in the exterior. You'll usually find that people who are manifesting their beloved are rolling up their sleeves and mucking it out in the world, or else they're sick. Both are ways of working it [the shadow] out in the collective.

As Elana explained, if the person were manifesting the high self in the mundane world, the dark side of their low self would not be unconscious, instead it would manifest in the world (interacting fields) around them as conditions of others needing attention, or it would manifest as their own sickness. Either would give the saint a chance to work through his dark self.

Trepidation

The last thing the group did on Friday was discuss logistics for the part of Saturday's initiation that would take place out in the desert.

> Elana: [It's about] fifteen minutes by car. I want most of you blindfolded, but some of you have to drive. [laughter]

Voices: Blindfolded!

Carla: Can you say anything about rattlesnakes? I've never had that experience.

[participant laughter]. What do you —-

Participant; [to others] Sh!

Elana: You hear a rattle. You become very still, and try to find where the snake is. Generally they're not going to bother you. You just find out where they are and you just send a heart and it's a cinch. Say the heart mantra and raise the heart to your third eye and then you say "excuse me" and leave.

[chatter]

Elana: I've almost stepped on them. I've stepped right over them and I've never been hurt. Oh, we forgot the snakebite kit! Maybe we should—

Participants: [In unison] I've got some. I've got one.

Elana: Thank you. We don't necessarily want anybody to become sick.

Regena: There's something else.

Elana: There are not going to be any rattlers out there.

Regena: There's something else. If you get bit, don't move. Just call for help because the more you move the more you circulate the poison.

Elana: Right, I've been coming out there for how many years now? I've been coming out there for seventeen years. I have for food and there wasn't any. Connie had looked in her bag several times and there was none. I said out loud, "I wish my beloved would give me an apple."

Connie: No, you said, "Beloved, please bring me an apple." [Connie was a herbalist, a woman in early middle age whom I had gotten to know the first session.]

[Laughter]

Participant: It wasn't that bad. [more laughter] Connie picked up her purse, stuck her hand in, and said "Here" [as she handed over the apple].

[Loud group laughter]

The group entertained the idea that the participant manifested the apple.

Vision Quest Meditation

Before closing on Saturday night, the group discussed at length how the time on Sunday should be spent. As before, Elana asked the participants what they would prefer to do. After much conversation about where and when to have lunch, how early to go to the desert for a meditation quest, which cars should be taken, where they should be parked, and the suggestion that whatever Elana wanted to do would be fine with participants, the group decided to postpone lunch until after closing at 3:00 to insure time for teaching.

On Sunday Elana taught more about the directions and the neters associated with them in preparation for the vision quest. She also taught never been bitten by a rattlesnake.

Participant: How many did you meet?

Elsa: I'm terrified of them. I really am.

Elana: Where we're going it's really safe. For those of you who are going around the rocks, all we have to worry about is quicksand and big—

Participants chatter: Let's clarify here.

And blindfolded drivers!

If you see a snake, run to the other side of the quicksand.

[laughter]

Elana: What do you say to the snake? Now remember these words. [repeats mantra]

Here mystery participants came equipped with a sense of adventure as well as a sense of humor. In the dialogue above Elana piqued the participants' adventurousness with comments about possible dangers countered with assurances that the outing would not really be risky. Participants responded jokingly. This sequence exemplifies participants' playfulness at mystery school.

Bonding with Beloved

After a brief period of teaching in the morning, initiation in the desert took all day Saturday. When participants received their beloved neters, mine turned out to be Amon, the hidden god, contained in Amon-Ra, the sun god. I suspected that I had already bonded with my neter the morning of the third weekend when the sun had warmed in such a particular way.

On Saturday evening participants shared past and present experiences surrounding the initiation.

> Katherine: I just realized as I was lying in bed last night. I was trying to have some kind of . . . experience and so I just kind of let all that go and that sign of a five pointed star from my neter, I just kind of acknowledged that. [Katherine was a junior executive with a well-known service corporation.] This morning I was sitting at breakfast. Joe was talking about [geological] continental plates and it was wonderful because I'm fascinated with that stuff. All of a sudden I saw that star floating in the air and I just said, "Oh, that was from the high self," because my stuff is stirring.

> [Joyous laughter from participants.]

> Katherine: I don't know, but the neter came. I'm just filled. I am. But it's just such a great joy, truly [in awe].

> Joe: Well, doesn't anybody want to hear a lecture on tectonic plates?

> [More loud laughter]

> Elana: I'll talk to you later! [More laughter]

> Participant: I had been snooping around last night because I was still hungry. I couldn't figure out why, but I was. I was in the room and I thought, "I really crave an apple. God, I'd love an apple." Connie and I had just destroyed the room looking

a practice for moving the *so* through the body. [It was similar to my dream.]

Designated drivers drove far out in the desert and parked the cars, releasing participants to scatter and find their spot for a two-hour meditation alone. Elana had suggested that each one sense the direction they should take. Once we found our special spot, we were to make a drawing of the holy city symbol on the ground, and sit in north, south east, west, and center to see what communications we might receive from the neters.

Later, back at the motel restaurant waiting for lunch to be ready, a group of holakunas sat in the padded chairs around a table in the bar and discussed their quest experiences. Ron, man in his thirties who was going through a divorce, looked very different than he had before the quest. His face was flushed and soft and his eyes shining.[2] Ron said he had gone north a short distance and then sat down. A bee buzzed around him and he thought of the girl he met last year. She had helped him to understand love. He remembered she had said bees were messengers of love. Then he thought how people wanting love were like bees. They sure wanted the honey, but they hated the idea of being stung. One had to overcome the fear of the sting. That was pretty good, he said, for a teaching from such a barren desert.

Participants were able to transcend the mundane in this initiation and experience something of the high self as their beloved neter. Some clear changes took place, as with Ron. The experience was, for

Fig. 5.1 Initiates head out into the desert on their quests.

many, awe producing. For all, the whole desert weekend was a grand adventure.

Journal entries: May 22, 1988. Elana had asked us to chant the throat mantra with the name of our neter one hundred thousand times during the interim between the fifth and sixth mystery school sessions. My university schedule was heavy that semester, with little time available for chanting mantras. Consequently I counted the paces from my usual parking spot to my office building on campus. Each morning I chanted the throat mantra silently with every step of the way.

On the morning of May 18 I stopped at the library to return a book before reaching the office. There I encountered a fellow graduate student and we chatted for a moment about the rigors of the anthropological linguistics class we were both taking. I began to see a blur around her head, and kept blinking because I thought my eyesight was blurring. Instead of going away the blur grew into a white glow extending out two or three inches around her body, with a pointed flare atop the head. Holakunas call this experience "seeing the aura." I had only seen auras a few times before, mostly when I was in deep trance. I was very surprised to see one at the library.

In a recent dream I saw my low self body. It was a dark shadow body shorter than my physical height. Out of the forehead rose a cobra made of totally clear rock crystal, alive and moving.

May 28, 1988 I dreamed I saw a figure forming in the sky toward the center of a dark evening cloud. It was a shape like an angel, but dark blue. Instead of bird wings she had butterfly-like wings. Looking at the figure in the dream thrust me into deeper and deeper trance states. Immediately I wondered what neter she might be and what was happening to me with the deepening trance. Then I woke up. It was morning.

From time to time for several weeks after the fifth weekend I felt a tingling in the top of my head that seemed to be energy bouncing around inside my head, needing to be released through the top of the skull. I hoped it was not something worse, and hoped Elana was going to open participants heads more or do something to end this phenomenon.

The Sixth Weekend: Sound, Dismemberment, and Change

The sixth session in June of 1988 dealt with the further opening of the throat chakra, shamanic dismemberment, power animals, channeling neters, and techniques for working with energies of creation, preservation, and destruction. A new addition to the conference room at Paloma, a carved piece resembling a ladder, topped the post. This seemed to represent climbing to the higher self. A wall hanging depicted Nepthes with blue skin and a gold dress against a dark blue background. I wondered if the blue skinned figure in my dream was Nepthes. There were also two large pictures of Egyptian painted eyes hanging on the sidewall.

Alterations

After opening circle Elana spoke of Khas:

There are two sounds, generalities, dictates, or tyrants that people live under all the time. (1) There is something wrong with me, there really is and if you do not believe it I'll prove it to you. (2) I'm separate from ____ (e.g. everything else). My senses tell me that I'm a separate sensory base.

92

She said that in this session we would enter these complexes directly through initiation, sound, ritual, love, and altered states to disrupt these habits. They were simply a way of living beyond fear of the irrational and the chaotic, for the high self appears irrational and chaotic because it is not logical, and this is threatening.[3] She said:

> In this [school] we have done a lot of practices, a lot of things that have caused altering, altering consciousness, coming in and creating a change with the tools that come to here [the throat chakra]. From here we begin to make that [altering] a part of our subconscious mind so that they are going on all the time. That brings awareness. It's not the practice that is important. The practice is just focusing the finger, the direction, to begin to engage the senses in a much larger capability: extrasensory perception. We are making the ordinary extraordinary.

Carla reported that a prominent line in her left palm had changed its position. In palmistry the left hand represents the propensities an individual is born with. The right hand shows what they have done with these abilities and opportunities. She perceived that when the line changed, she virtually changed her life history in a previous incarnation. Elana explained:

> When you have suffered you've got quantum principles to apply to your life, and not textbook mythology. You are the master of time because you have gone beyond it. Therefore, past and future, the

linear sequences have no meaning. You change your past all the time. You go backwards and forwards.

Elana talked about her own process of shamanic dismemberment, which manifested in illness when she realized that the world that had been described to her by others was nothing but cardboard, and there was nothing behind it.

On that Friday evening Elana required participants to make their own sound of pain and anguish. We formed a circle and one at a time went to the center to let out our sound. Some screamed, others yelled or groaned, some choked and coughed. After the sound was heard the group repeated it over continuously until it transformed into a musical tone, expressing harmony, even joy. The change seemed to be an unthinking process in which each individual could hardly tolerate the discordance of forty people screaming or groaning. They naturally sought harmony. As the sound became harmonic, I could not distinguish my own voice from the others as I sang.

On Saturday participants learned many practices and went through a very long initiation that involved shamanistic death and dismembering. At one point in this initiation Elana came to each participant to open the top of their head through psychic surgery. During the dance that followed the initiates danced their power animal, the animal that represents their lower self. Larry set up a strobe light and all danced in the flicker of the universe.

Channeling Neters

Participants were instructed to form a circle. One person at a time was to go to the center and asked for channeling from the neters. Channeling is a process in which a spirit entity expresses itself through a practitioner's body using voice, writing, or body movements to communicate with humans. Elana instructed, "Go out and tell the group what you need and then the person that can give the sacred speech, that can give the answer, the channeling, do it."

During the channeling the neters revealed events from Marsha's previous incarnation in medieval Japan that had bearing on her current life situation. Marsha began to process, to release the emotional and spiritual energy blocks, and she began to gag. The group decided it would help her clear the blocks if she could vomit. She could not. A basin was brought and the musicians struck up discordant vomiting music with a vomiting drumbeat. The other participants began an impromptu vomiting dance, in which they pantomimed the act, but none of this moved Marsha to vomit. (Later, however Marsha developed other physical symptoms, which accomplished the purge.) The next day Lisa remarked that now she realized that even vomiting could be a ritual.

Sunday morning my cabin mates discussed the channeling. They agreed that Rudolph and Nancy were "true channels." Rudolph and Nancy did not seem to know what they had said and their voices and body language had changed. There were others who seemed truly possessed, but some holakunas' channeling seemed to have been influenced by their middle selves. This was less authentic.

That Sunday Elana spoke of participants' sacred marriage with their beloved. She said it meant participants were to actually become the beloved. Males should find something feminine and wear it and meditate on being females. It could be hidden, like a chain. Women were to do the same with the masculine.

Participants were instructed to make a ritual mask representing their finest spiritual qualities and empower it with their high self.

Bridges and Doorways

A dialogue session followed. A participant commented, saying she dreamed Sunday morning that she looked at her scalp and there were three holes in it. Elana replied that yes, she had made three holes in the crown. Participants must be careful not to let others touch their head. Christy told of her dream the night before the musical group gave a concert (May 24, 1988) in which they chanted the Holakuna mantras with Elana's permission). She said:

As I went to sleep—I had spent a week of many hours chanting—I was seeing blue, misty blue and looking up and was seeing the underbelly of this great insect. The sounds that this insect was making were extraordinary. I have no words to describe it. They weren't like, pleasing. I noticed that there was a stream coming out from this being and going into my throat. It at first looked like strobe [light]. I zeroed in to see what it was, and it was skulls. They weren't human, and this is very similar. [She referred to a tiny skull carved from bone that Elana had given each participant to wear on a black band at the throat.]

Elana said the strobe teaches that the world is a flicker. Annette commented that she had an experience years ago with the flicker. While watching a movie her perception shifted into a mode in which she was seeing the blank spaces between the frames. What was happening?

Elana responded:

That is a doorway[4] and you can learn to hold the blank. You can learn to hold the blank through breath work and then you are a master of contraction and expansion. It's a bridge.

She said that Western culture does not offer any training except shamanistic and mystical training about how to live in the world. Instead we have instruction on how to go away from the world. The experience of living in the world could be overwhelming. The way the world works is not logical. The neters and Holakuna symbols are bridges, avenues of focus, to help make sense out of what is really there.

Virginia noted that her power animal was a cat and she is allergic to cats.

Elana responded, "You react to your own Power?" (laughter) "Any kind of allergy indicates what is threatening in the world."

Ron said that he seemed to have two power animals.[5] Elana said that if you had two power animals, your life was in tremendous conflict. But your power animal could change.

Following this dialogue the group received instruction in working with creative, preservative, and destructive forces. The session ended with a circle, as usual.

Holy Family Business

During the third, fourth, and fifth sessions I had occasionally come upon certain participants, especially Zelda and women from the San Francisco Bay Area, saying things like, "Well, it's just not right." And "She should know better than that." I was not able to find out whom they were talking about. Before the sixth weekend a letter came from Zelda saying that as a representative of a group of participants and with Elana's permission she had written Sally, requesting that she either change her behavior or drop out of mystery school. The objectionable behavior was inconsiderate "farting and belching," which upset those sitting near Sally in the crowded room. Elana said she deplored that this should happen, yet she allowed Zelda to follow her conscience in the matter. I did not know Sally and had not been aware of the problem.

Sally had notified Elana that she would not return, saying that she was bothered by the lack of structure and organization in the mystery school. Some of the other participants commiserated with Sally and urged others to give her support, but Sally chose to stay out. There were no further requests that anybody leave. Apparently the Holakuna family had purged itself.

During the fourth, fifth, and sixth sessions of mystery school the alternate reality had been well established through the joint efforts of

Elana and participants. They had cooperated in a psychological journey beginning in the participants' childhoods that attempted to change embodied memories of early experience and bond to parent figures, to bond with the group as their family, and to bond with their beloved neter as adult lover and high self. This was done through using archetypical figures, the neters in visualizations including shamanistic initiations and through psychic surgery, chanting mantras, and immersion in sound.

Various participants experienced the opening and development of extrasensory capacities, communications from their low selves and the neters, synchronicities, and physical changes. They shared their experiences with each other. Both teacher and participants expressed dissatisfaction with a Western reality characterized as mass consciousness, nothing but cardboard, as well as Western societal systems and trends (childrearing, major religions, and new age disciplines).

Notes

1. Elana required all participants to give her a computer generated astrological birth chart after the first session of mystery school. Upon participants' request she gave them each a copy of her birth chart.

2. According to Felicitas D. Goodman, changes in the body are observable in individuals undergoing the altered states of consciousness known as religious trance, namely: deep breathing, profuse perspiring, blushing, trembling, or twitching (1988).

3. Communications from the high self are likely to be symbolic or

metaphoric, rather than logical. A significant genre of literature in the Twentieth Century, science fiction, has dealt extensively with the idea that the divine is chaotic. Arthur C. Clarke's *Childhood's End* is exemplary.

4. A doorway is a means of moving beyond mundane reality into an alternative reality.

5. Here Elana used the term "power animal" to denote the one animal that symbolizes or encapsulates a Holakuna's low self, also referred to as the totem animal by holakunas. "Power animal" can also refer to animals whose spirits are allies, spirit helpers that do not symbolize the holakuna's low self.

Chapter 6 Embodying the High Self

Journal entry: August 27, 1988. On August 23, I dreamed I saw my face reflected in a mirror. It was my most beautiful, radiant and whole face, smiling back at me. Standing beside me was Elana smiling joyfully and also reflected in the mirror, which she was holding. On August 7 a former lover appeared in my dreams. He held up a mirror for me to look into. My image was a lion with a full mane.

During the interim between the sixth and seventh sessions I made my ritual mask of fabric sewn onto a wire frame. As I finished the red eyes, the mask became a little disturbing. In its presence I felt somebody was looking at me. I decided this presence could only be benevolent, following my intention in making the mask. Months later when my grown daughter slept in a room with my mask, she dreamed twice that strange teachers came to her wearing it.

The Seventh Weekend: Third Eye, Clear Consciousness

Initiations and practices took up most of the seventh session of mystery school (in September of 1989), with little lecturing, but more question and answer periods than on previous weekends. The session began on Friday with a powerful initiation in which participants became one with Sekhmet, the neter of pure force, pure energy, and pure consciousness, personified as a lion headed goddess. Was this what my lion headed dream was about?

Elana taught about ten bodies: the astral body, the mental body, the double, the emotional body, the physical body, the causal body, the personality, the etheric/dreaming body, the immortal spirit, and the life force body. The mystery school was helping its participants build their ten bodies. She said:

> Our conscious mind is this little tip of the iceberg. The mental body and the dreaming body go way, way down. As you go deeper and deeper into the dreaming body you go deep, deep, into the shade and what you find are these fourteen doors, fourteen star powers. This is why we have to go through the dark, why we go through the iconoclasts: the ones that challenge our barriers, that which brings up every system and makes known to us what is there through self-knowledge.

I understood Elana to mean that it is those who reject the icons of their era (the socially deviant?) who can reach the high self. They confront the dark contents of their own unconscious as part of the mystical journey. The power of the high self is subtle energy, emanating from the stars. The holakunas learned to use fourteen different types of it

102

that weekend. "Beyond everything", Elana said, "is Sekhmet, the principle of clear consciousness, the vital force. She is beyond personality, khas and emotions. Hers is the power of the third eye (sixth chakra, direct perception and compassion)."

Before initiation into the third eye, truth telling which had been left incomplete at the closing of the sixth session was completed. Many of the participants' truths had to do with gender issues: remembering being a sexually abused child, becoming aware of their own sexism, revealing their own homosexuality. The truth tellers expressed a perception that mystery school had given them new awareness about these personal issues. Initiation into the third eye and the fourteen star energies took most of Saturday.

At one point Elana taught the initiates how to use Sekhmet energies for exorcism. She spoke of the meaning of exorcism:

Exorcism means to disrupt a fixed reality and make fluid that which is conditioned. It essentially entails moving from that which is the master program into the present moment because [otherwise] the past replicates into the future what it supposed liberation or freedom would be, when it just contains the same old thing in modified form, [sic.].

When Elana spoke of exorcism as the power of change and of a particular aspect of Sekhmet as devourer of karma, Carla had a realization about the changed line in her hand. Carla said:

My beloved neter is Sekhmet [devourer aspect]. I just put this all together, what happened in the desert weekend. I did the hundred thousand mantras with the beloved's name and that's when everything speeded up for me and I did it instantaneously. Then the lines in my hand changed . . . devouring karma. I didn't realize she [Sekhmet] did that.

During the free dance that followed the initiation this anthropologist found herself jumping up and down in an uncharacteristic way. For a long time I could not seem to stop. I felt that some power outside myself (probably Sekhmet) had entered me and was jumping my body up and down as if I were a puppet.

Masks, Robes, and Skits

Elana had divided the participants into groups of nine or ten. After the initiation each group produced a skit on creation, preservation and destruction, wearing their masks and robes, assuming their god self. All the masks were quite imaginative, and displayed peaceful benevolent expressions. Most were made of special plastic material that is applied on a piece of mesh molded into the shape of the individual's face. Some were bought and covered with feathers and sequins. Elsa's was of this type, a velvet mask made to look like an owl face. There was a paper maché mask of Anubis with amber plastic globes for eyes and silver lines on the ears. Some masks had horns. Paulene's had a gourd attached to the forehead at the third eye. In the end of the gourd she had inlaid a piece of polished hematite.[1] An Angel holding a smoking torch was painted on the body of the gourd.

Most participants had fashioned robes from the sheets they brought to mystery school. Many of these had been dyed black, blue, red, or purple, while a few were left white. Geometric elemental symbols and the ankh, representing embodied life energy, were appliqued or painted on them.

Some holakunas had chosen a different sort of robe. They bought silk robes, or obtained them from Ann, painted to order. Silk robes tended to be hip length and semicircular with a part of the hem stitched together on either side to form bat wing sleeves. Maureen's was purple with a fiery oriental dragon painted on the back. Annette was wearing a black t-shirt, which said in white letters, "Born a Kahuna." It sported a design of planets and nebula.

Sheet robes came in various styles. One had a hood and looked like a monk's habit. Another, fashioned with a yoke at the shoulders, resembled a choir robe. Several participants had made a hole in the middle of the sheet for their head, made sleeves, and belted the garment in front, passing the belt through holes in the sides to leave the back loose and full. Shoshona had not wanted to throw away any part of her sheet. She used every scrap cut from it in the fashioning and decoration of her robe.

Two of the skits took the form of interpretative dance, and two involved dialogue. One of the dialogues went something like this:

[Gods wandering aimlessly.] What to do?

Let's create a universe.

Again?

Shall we do galaxies and planets?

Animals, animals, animals. I want animals! [jumping up and down]

What about humans?

Oh, they make such a mess.

But they're cute when they get all upset and call on us.

Who's going to be the supreme god this time?

Oh no, not me!

Shall we let them have mystery schools?

Oh no, not mystery schools again!

After the skits, participants chanted the mantra for "I rest in Sekhmet" for several minutes. Then a spontaneous dance developed in which circle dancing and a row dance evolved. One individual after another would come forward and dance down between the rows doing a particular step they knew.

What to Tell Outsiders

At one point during the session participants discussed again how they would explain mystery school to people in their everyday lives.

Zelda: [to Elana] How is it when we go out in the world? What do we say to people?

Elana: Well you say it's a Huna empowerment into the Egyptian mysteries. A pre-Egyptian – you know we were having a discussion about what to actually say or how to describe [Holalkuna practice] because it's not Egyptian. It's pre-Egyptian. It's pre-dynastic, [with a tone of irony]. You try to convey that to the secular world – and Kahuna, of course, is associated with Polynesia, which was much later.

Elana talked about the significance of the word Huna. A participant commented that as soon as people hear the word Egyptian they have an idea of what that means which is incorrect.

Another participant. You mean Cleopatra?

Elana: Right, because the dynastic times were incredibly corrupt . . . What is it before dynastic, Atlantis? I mean good grief!

[Participant laughter]

Walt: Well I've been trying to solve that, working in a hospital. People want to know where I'm going for retreat. I tell them I'm doing a yearlong training in alternative healing approaches that spans – You know we've talked about shamans, the Egyptians, the works. . . [Walt was a thirty-six year old student in transpersonal psychology, planning to become a therapist.] Virginia: For people who are in the university it works very well to say that you're studying pre-dynastic Egyptian metaphysics, religion and healing.

Elana: Use the word pre-dynastic, because do you think the secular corporate world knows what pre-dynastic means?

Virginia: But, I mean, they at least know –

Elana: They know the word dynastic?

At lunch on Sunday participants seated at my table again discussed how much about mystery school they could reveal in their mundane lives. Ed, the psychiatrist, said that he had a traditional practice but he did whatever was appropriate. He did not talk about new age stuff professionally, but felt its influence was growing across the country. He mentioned practitioners who offered new age healing.

Someone quipped, "I guess you won't show up in the office tomorrow with your headband." (Participants had discussed headbands as a way of putting the appropriate symbol over the third eye for specific practices.) Ed said no, he would not, but he did wear the skull neckband. He wore it under his tie, but in his office he took off his tie. Nancy remarked that she got questions about the skull bead, noting that people were prying for information. I said that I wore my skull neck bead to my university classes and got questions from graduate students.

Bi-Location: Containing the Paradox

Later, with the whole group, some participants mentioned their experience of bi-location during Saturday's initiation, their perception of being in two places at the same time.

Marsha: [to Elana] You know my third eye followed you around the room. I was gone. All of a sudden I realized it was following you around the room.

108

Elana: That's great. You track someone and you have telepathic communication of all fourteen levels, using the fourteen energies.

Another participant: Well I noticed that I was seeing myself from over here and over here during some of the initiation. It was like I was watching you guys, [Larry and Elana]. Then I was wondering, well who's here? [Indicates her own position.]

[Participant laughter]

Elana: I would say that probably it was your double. You are experiencing it in your master program. Then your master program is distinguishing itself from your other bodies so that you can be – The minute you can bi-locate you've contained the paradox.

Gender

The session ended with discussion of whether or not a mystery school for women only should be held the next year. Paul spoke against this, saying that now was a period of processing for both men and women in the same time and the same place and the same energy.

Carla, who had always before been a strong advocate for women taking back their power, said:

I'm much more whole and healthy now than I've ever been in my life. I feel I'm capable of moving into attempting a balance, and finding friendship and love with men. I've not been able to experience that until now.

Walt interjected that thanks to all the women at mystery school he was now wearing bracelets. Elana called for a devouring of stereotypes by Sekhmet. The group chanted the "Sekhmet devouring" mantra for several minutes. As the chanting faded out someone said, "Thank you."

Katherine said, "I love you all!"

Others repeated, "Yes, me too." Chatter rose as the group disbanded.

The Eighth Weekend: Crown Chakra

The eighth level in October of 1988 was the weekend for opening the crown chakra, bringing a closer relationship with the high self. The Paloma conference room was decorated differently. Instead of the usual neter hanging, two Egyptian eyes hung above the altar. A silk painting of a winged female with a sun disk upon her head, Sekhmet, was suspended over one of these eyes. Another silk scarf depicting Maat, goddess/principle of absolute truth, highest justice, and mercy, hung to the left of the altar.

The altar was set up as usual, but behind it was a surrealistic picture showing a canyon full of water that became the robe of a practitioner who wore a strange pointed cap. The earth on either side of the canyon became the sky of another world, decorated with an eye (Sekhmet) on the left and a feather (Maat) on the right of the practitioner. From among the stars the practitioner reached into the sky of this world. Energy like lightening emitted from his/her hands and touched an ankh enclosed in a circle situated above a desert landscape.

Learning the Mysteries

Elana was ill that weekend, suffering from fever and chills, but she went ahead with the session. Much of the teaching during that eighth weekend was incomprehensible to me, the sort of teaching that one can experience, but not describe. In her preview on Friday evening Elana presented the idea of *hunadity*, a state of joy, ascension, inseparability of all things, learning through living, living in the moment, and supernal regeneration. She instructed participants to think about not having any points of reference. She said, quoting a popular satirical theater group, "Everything you know is wrong."

One sign of hunadity was the shaking or trembling that participants including myself sometimes experienced at mystery school. This shaking indicated that the actual cells in the body were changing. Hunadity might happen only when a person was in love, because that might be the only time they were not self-centered. Elana stated that we needed to be in love with everyone.

Elana also taught of metaphorical dragons called *shabin* and of *uraeii*, the familiar snakes. These creatures open different doors to non-ordinary reality[2] or life opportunity as they weave the tapestry of existence.

Wands of Attention

The third major new teaching was that of the five wands or scepters representing states of attention: waking, dreaming, dreamless sleep, pure joy, and all enduring serenity of awareness. In this context Elana said that waking consciousness is the real dream from which Holakunas must

111

awaken. (Reminiscent of my dream of the blue lady with butterfly wings.) Each of these five states corresponded to a particular wand, which Elana described in detail. Participants were urged to make wands after they returned home.

Anubis

On Saturday morning Lisa asked the group if anybody had heard the coyotes howling during the night. A few participants indicated that they had, but most had heard nothing.

Elana said, "Are you sure they were on this plane?" She reminded Lisa of all the times she had said she could not do this "stuff" (psychic awareness).

Lisa said she thought the whole community would wonder what was happening during the night, the howling was so loud. Some participants said they heard coyotes in the distance, maybe twenty miles away. Others said they heard a woman screaming.

Lisa said, "That's similar to what I heard. It would start out like a woman screaming and then turn into a coyote sound. It was like a scream and then laughter." Marsha asked everyone who heard the coyotes to hold up their hand. About five people responded. Then she asked all those who had Anubis[3] as their neter, or had some connection with Anubis to raise their hand. (Anubis is the Jackal-headed neter of time, which brings death, and the protector of eternity.) The same individuals responded. Jill and Lisa were the only people in this group with Anubis for their beloved neter, but the others had names, totem animals, or

112

dreams linking them to Anubis. Then someone mentioned the friendly wolf dog that had tried repeatedly to get into the conference room that morning. I too had seen the half-wolf dog. I never saw it before or after that day, although the Paloma staff said it lived nearby.

Elana said:

Well there are some that might have heard them but whether there was a coyote or not, it was still Anubis. And there's no distinction, but you [affiliated with Anubis] are on that frequency and therefore you can pick it up, and they may have been very far away. . . . There may have been no coyotes on this plane at all . . . any number of combinations. It's a real good exercise just to look at it, argue it or think it all the way through from each one of those [perspectives] and make each true.

On Saturday evening Elana began the crown chakra initiation. Later she said that she was so ill that she had to break off this initiation before it was complete and do a second installment on Sunday. Many participants experienced either falling asleep or forgetting everything that took place during the initiation. Elana said this was because hunadity and higher states of mind attained in the initiation put demands on the central nervous system so unusual for normal consciousness that it would rather turn off by going to sleep than deal with them.

The Saturday segment of the crown chakra initiation ended with each participant discovering the power animal that represented his or her high self and depicting that animal in free dance. Participants received an "animal head" placed over their head because in order to enter into their higher self, they needed to go through animal consciousness, which holakunas believe is a very high state of consciousness. Elana and Carla spoke about and handed out information for the animal rights movement.

There was a long sharing period before continuation of the initiation on Sunday. Elana said she had to know "Where everybody was" before she could continue. Some people had not found or at least not recognized their high self animal. Jill reported:

When it came time for an animal to appear none came to me either. . . . I went over and asked Elana at the end. She said it was a cat. Then last night I had nightmares all night long where . . . a patient turned into a cat and wouldn't let me catch it. I woke up in -- just pain. Then when I fell asleep again I had a big dog, a boxer, attack me and maim me. Then the person who owned the dog said I was in the dog's space after all, to leave it. Can you give me some insight as to what my animal was or what's happening?

Elana responded:

The dream is very interesting and only you can know what it means. What occurs to me . . . was that you were in sacred space and you weren't in it. That kind of judgment comes around because Anubis keeps the space sacred and doesn't allow people into the space unless they are "in the space" to be in the space [In the appropriate state of mind, body, spirit, or emotion to reach the consciousness required for the initiation]. That's the function of Anubis. Also

114

Anubis is the devourer that carries you into death. Oftentimes a dream of Anubis means the death of a part of the consciousness. Not being able to catch the cat reveals to me that you weren't able to get into that part of the consciousness you really wanted to be in. The cat represents power.

Healing

Throughout this session participants engaged in healing each other. I walked into my room on Saturday to find a healing in progress. Connie, my roommate was working with Alice, who was telling of betrayal by her mother in childhood. Alice was punished for something she hadn't done because her father was convinced of her guilt, although her mother knew she was innocent. Alice felt her mother's betrayal related to her adult habit of constantly protecting her integrity. Connie related a similar experience from her teen years. Alice told how somebody hit her car with a rock, denting it, and her husband would not believe her story, assuming she was covering up for an accident. Her mother, who was in the car at the time, told a story so different from Alice's version that it upheld her husband's suspicions.

Both initiates concluded that women will lie and allow their children to be debased in order to placate their husbands' suspicions. Connie said that this frequently happens in child abuse and Alice's experience amounted to abuse. She suggested Alice needed to heal her ancestors seven generations back using the appropriate Holakuna mantra. Alice mentioned some of her grandparents gender related conflicts that required healing.

Most of the healing practices I observed took place on long breaks between meals or before school began in the morning. Mornings, Vanessa was usually in the center rear of the conference room with her tarot cards spread out on the carpet giving a combined tarot reading and counseling session to some participant. During a long break on Sunday, I observed Larry working on Julie, who was lying stretched out on the floor. He was passing his hands above her body, perhaps doing the Holakuna scanning practice. Another participant was teaching Helen and two others a movement that resembled belly dancing. Lisa was giving Christy a big hug. Katherine was doing a head to knee yoga posture by herself.

A Synchronicity

When Elana had suggested that participants should make wands, Walt had already begun. He told me he admired the wands offered for sale in rock shops but could not afford them. On a "ritual weekend" in the wilderness he found several pieces of natural wood near his campsite. At home he realized that these would make good wands. He obtained crystals to "fit the personality of the wands" and found ways to attach them to the sticks.

One day he went to a private home to look at crystals on sale there. The owner's boyfriend picked up Walt's snake wand and put it down quickly because of the "overwhelming energy" in it. This led to conversation with the owner about working on relationships and going between various states of consciousness. Walt agreed to make an "inter-dimensional wand to help the owner in her meditations." After she chose the crystal that would tip the wand, they performed a ritual on the spot to "initiate" the crystals and the stick to her "energy and personality". When he completed the wand she placed it on her altar. That same month I happened to be in a local shaman shop in Eugene, Oregon where I observed a man showing the storeowner a metal wand fitted with a quartz crystal and some semiprecious stones. Conversation revealed that he had just begun making wands.

Walt said he did not know these events related to mystery school until the current weekend. In addition to wands of attention, mystery school was dealing with snakes and shabin with fire energies. He realized the wands he was making were a shabin and a snake wand. This was synchronicity. "I suppose somehow I was intuiting what was going to come up and building a set of shamanistic equipment," he commented.

Difficulties

On Sunday there was sharing of the difficulties participants had been having with the empowerments and teaching that weekend. Rudolph said that he had been feeling, "Oh gee, I don't want to be here. I think these practices are stupid." When he said that he was OK with that because he had seen it before, there were chuckles from the group. Rudolph said he had sworn during the third mystery school weekend he would never come back and yet here he was.

Christy: I feel that last session was so powerful. To me what

117

was powerful about it was that everything we did and everything you taught us seemed to relate to everything else you were saying and had said. I experienced spontaneous awakening of insight that was doors opening, that opened doors that opened more doors, opening more doors. . . . I thought, "This is how it's supposed to be."

That has not been present for me in this session. I have experienced – it felt more like a hodge-podge rather than a congruence. I didn't feel like there was that growing, building upon. I was feeling growing aggravation myself because of that. One of the last practices we did felt so much out of the now, trying to do all those things, that at a certain point I opened my eyes so I could see the floor and part of my body and just let that be what was now.

Elana: A couple of things are going on here. One is that those states are very difficult to enter into. [She went on to talk of how she herself had felt ill during the teaching.]

. . . We are leaving everything behind here. The purpose now that we have is to free ourselves from the powers that we've gained. Do you understand what I mean?

Participants:

Mm hum.

Yes.

No!

Elana: It's very hard for me to express because the physical mind simply is not there with the capacity of retention.

Ed: When people are presented with information which strains and pushes aside their normal way of doing things they do get angry and frustrated. In this role they have to, in order to expand and develop more neural tracks.

Elana: Especially in that practice [Referred to by Christy]. I hesitate to even give these practices out. Every mystery school [session] I say, "I'm never going to do this again." I have to tell you that's how I feel too. I'm never going to do this. It isn't worth it. I just want to teach beginning classes. Each time it is really wonderful what begins to happen afterwards.

Ruth: If I hadn't had the breakthrough with the will [third chakra] I would have felt exactly like Christy. I've been in this stuff for thirty years. That's the hardest lesson I've ever come up against, the idea that this is all dreaming. You hear it intellectually, but to get it into the marrow of your bones is almost impossible. . . .It was totally foreign when you kept saying it was dreaming. . . That was difficult.

Elana: I think it was one of the most difficult passages and still is for me. Sometimes it makes me feel psychotic and enraged at my teachers, absolutely enraged.

Elana ended the closing circle with, "Let every person you are with be the center of the universe. We are one. We stay linked in between [sessions] and next time we will enter the Neith."

There was a definite shift in the character of the mystery school experience at the eighth weekend. Once more participants had difficulty interpreting the teachings, initiations and their effects. Elana made it clear that conducting mystery school was hard for her too. And that the opening of the seventh chakra had been a difficult passage. The unbidden manifestation of Anubis was a bit unnerving.

Notes

1.   Hematite is an iron ore. Hunas and new age adherents obtain the crystalline type, a metallic crystal. I have seen it used in jewelry with rose quartz and other natural stone.

2. Nonordinary reality is a term Carlos Castaneda used in his Don Juan series. Elana used this term and often referred to Castaneda's books, chiefly to note similarities between Don Juan's (supposed) teaching and her own.

3. Jackals are old world wild dogs, smaller than a wolf, with habits similar to coyotes. Participants knew that a dog or wolf appearing in visions and/or real life could be a messenger from Anubis, or the principle of Anubis himself.

Chapter 7 Everything You Know is Wrong

Participants were now well aware of their high selves, having become familiar with seven chakras in the past year. Difficult as the eighth weekend had been, for many participants the teachings and initiations of this ninth session proved to be even harder to understand and remember. This was the last weekend for anthropological research according to my agreement with Elana. The tenth meeting of the mystery school, to be held the following year, was billed as a reunion.

The Ninth Weekend: Entering the Void

This weekend (December of 1988) we continued accessing the high self with Neters Neith and Maat, whose likenesses were on display in the conference room. Neith is the void, the unborn one, principle of the infinite divine, the self-sustaining and self-existent principle of life that is secret, unknown, and all pervading. She is the weaver who weaves the fabric of existence. Elana's instruction, again difficult to comprehend and communicate, centered on experiencing the void. The session began with a practice in which participants mentally went through all the chakras, which were now open and aligned.

Perfection

Elana lectured on hunanidy. She said:

In the end the very impediment to realizing ourselves and awakening the truth, the obstacle to the ultimate is knowledge and power. Where there is knowledge there is no wisdom, because knowledge obscures it.

. . .You are already a high self body, you are already a Buddha. . . . Our model that we look up to for guidance, that model is the very thing that causes . . . the inability for the realization of our perfection. It's not the world that is an illusion, It's you who are an illusion. The problem that is the root and core of all our problems is that we exist at all.

She urged participants to begin to acknowledge the perfection that already exists, asking them, seated in a circle to share the ways they each denied their perfection.

Zelda: I worry and try to control too much and that is what gets in my way.

Elana: So you need to worry and control until it's enjoyable.

[Participant laughter.]

Participant: That is getting a nervous breakdown.

Elana: Break down, good. That's it. Breakdown because that's the breaking down of the center that is the false center.

[Later.]

Ron: Well I've got a lot better since the class started about being happy, accepting myself.

Elana: That always makes something attractive or repulsive.

Ron: Wishing things were different.

Elana: Yes, exactly.

Ron: I do a lt less of that now.

Elana: If they [things] were different what would they be like?

Ron: Well then probably something else . . . to bitch about.

Elana: Ah, thank you. So just carry on.

[Participant laughter]

[Later]

Ann: I feel like—What was the question?

[laughs with participants.] So I have the answer. You know that about self-esteem and perfection -— I thought this is what I do.

Elana: This is what you do.

Ann: Try to get it right.

Elana: Bingo!

Ann: If I do [get it right] then I can judge that and if I don't I get to judge that.

Elana: Exactly.

Ann: The thing where I put a lot of my attention when I'm not here, when I'm out in the world is in doing and in keeping busy. Also now I'm amazed at the number of goals I can write.

I have a lot of goals.

Elana: What is the major way that they keep from happening. How can you prevent them?

Ann: Waiting for them to happen rather than just doing them.

Elana: Judging again. If you do it right they'll happen and if you—I want you to know that when you're in your truth, which you were when you laughed, at that moment the most extraordinary means comes about for you to realize that goal, any goal, because there's no longer obstruction. The trying to achieve is actually what is getting in your way.

Later Elana asked for feedback about the "ways I deny my perfection" sharing session, (above) explaining:

I don't want to be totally unclear because I feel like everything that I'm saying is making perfect sense. Another thing, too, when you go into confusion you can't file something away in the same old filing cabinets [neural tracks]. . . .

Zelda: This is what I experienced when you told me to go ahead and worry and try to control. What I ended up coming to was dreaming, speaking out loud in my sleep. Rick woke me up. I was speaking out loud and I was saying [the reabsorbing energy mantra]. I was kind of screaming it. I was just saying enough, enough, it's OK just the way it is. It's an illusion. The whole thing is an illusion. [Referring to a family problem]

Elana: You're an illusion. It's not an illusion. There's

something that happened. . . .The tree still falls in the forest.

Healing Across the Void

On Saturday the group did a healing practice in which they selected the appropriate energy and beamed it to another in the circle. I beamed energy to Zelda, and did not look at Lisa, who was sending energy to me. I was aware that a muscle pain I'd had in my right hip for two weeks was slowly dissipating. When the healing was finished the pain was completely gone. Later Lisa told the group of her experience healing me:

I was looking at her and seeing a lot of blocked energy around her throat and her feet. So with my [types of energy] I was inserting the energy closer and closer inside of her so that "gook" started dissolving and then doing it in other parts of her body, particularly around the womb. . . . Then what happened once there was room, the [energy] became like bands of light. It really embraced her completely.

The message for her was, holding her and embracing her saying, "you're so important, you don't even have to struggle to keep on telling yourself you're important. It was easy to see it healing her, but it was also tuning into my issues and healing me.

Elana pointed out that this was the first time Lisa had ever admitted to psychic "seeing". Throughout mystery school Lisa had been asking for more tactile, auditory and scent cues during Elana's guided visualization exercises in order to more completely realize the imagery. The visual cues were insufficient for her.

The above instance demonstrated Holakuna healing at work. The healing involved both channeling specific energies plus a channeled message directed at the mental/emotional energy blocks, namely my "hang-up" about my importance which was very real to me. It possibly manifested in the hip pain. Both "hang-up" and hip pain seemed to lessen following Lisa's ministration. Practitioner and client were being healed, but beyond that, all the people I interacted with in mundane life were touched by my concern over my importance.

Playfulness

During a long break on Saturday I came into the conference room early and found seven people stretched out on the floor in yoga corpse pose. Shoshona and Paul were standing and embracing. Walt was standing in the Holakuna pose of the ankh. Three other participants hinted that Walt's belly was rather prominent in that stance, and should be tickled. He settled for a back rub instead. Later Judy tied around her head two silk scarfs with Egyptian eyes [painted by Ann] situating the painted eyes over her own eyes.

On Sunday, before lecture, part of a tape recording of participants chanting mantras accidentally got played on fast speed. Shoshona and Marsha made jokes about the once popular "Chipmunks" songs, inventing titles: "The Chipmunks go to Egypt, The Chipmunks Speak in Tongues, The Chipmunks' Version of Current Mantras."

Communication from Animals

On the more serious side, several people reported unusual

experiences with animals after the eighth session. Christy told of the raccoon family living in the walls of her house. She had seen them and heard "spooky sounds" of baby raccoons scratching and rapping in the walls. Then one night a mother raccoon and her three babies appeared to Christy in a lucid dream. The mother said, "Feed my children."

Christy said, "I will." Thereafter the babies thumped at the door every day and Christy brought them food. Soon they were following at her feet. Now when she heard the scratching she knocked on the walls and the raccoons rapped back. The mother had not been seen since the dream. Elana suggested that perhaps the mother was off meditating. The participants laughed.

Christy added, "It's true that I'm opening and communicating with other species. When I teach [music] every animal that's around comes in for the lesson. Now it's really intense. I literally have to set up chairs for the cats." (Participants laughed.)

Elana related how while she was at home typing the assignment of meditation animals for the participants, a deer came up to the picture window and, putting its nose against the glass, stared at her. She tried to continue with her work but every time she moved, the deer moved, so she knew it was looking at her. "I knew he wanted my undivided attention," she said, "So I linked up with the third eye. We started to exchange. That was when I had the experience of my eyes wrapping around. He gave me his eyes." Elana had told us earlier that she had seen through the deer's eyes with a field of vision on either side of her head.

"These things start to happen when there's no division," she said. (I understood "no division" to mean a state of unity with the high self, hunadity, or being in the void where a person perceives herself as one with her environment.)

The discussion continued.

Participant: Do animals have a third eye?

Elana: Oh, yes, oh, very highly developed. Otherwise They couldn't function.

Same participant: So you link with their third eye?

Elana: Yes, you link with their third eye. Yes, definitely. All species have that. Then when the third eye opens [in people], that is the morphogenetic connection with the interspecies. Then cruelty to animals becomes overwhelming. See we are noticing it now from the third eye, which is simultaneously the opening of the heart. The cruelty that is thrust upon them becomes enormous. We just have to do something about it,

Lisa: I have a question. Animals have chakras like we do, connecting with the third eye and the heart?

Elana: Yes, they do.

Lisa: Then does a mountain? I would imagine that a mountain also has chakras.

Elana: The earth has chakras.

Lisa: The trees have chakras?

Elana: Yes, because the chakras are the vortex centers from

which emanate the aka, and so they exist everywhere as wheels within wheels within wheels. Some of them are more accessible to the conscious mind as they come through the gradients of density outward. As we go into geometries of mind with our mind and are astral projecting, whatever, then we have more access to them.

Elana told participants that in this way everything is imbued with a spirit. Holakuna's understanding of this principle was like the anthropologists term animism, except that anthropologists have used the term as a way of distancing themselves from primitive people. (Western scholars had defined life in a way that excluded rocks, clouds, stars etc., and considered their own knowledge superior.) "We can never study another people," Elana said. "We either are that people or not." She said that cultures with a belief system called animism were usually taboo bound. "We have a great way of condemning the secular world and the technological world," Elana said. "Actually I think we really need to look at that judgment because it [the technical world] frees us from the *endogeny* of so many taboos. Now we're becoming more aware of what we are doing."

> Lisa: Continuing on this could you also say that clouds have chakras which makes cloud gazing so powerful, and fire also has chakras which comes out with the . . .?
>
> Elana: Exactly—only they're like the chakras of the chakras. Because they're the elements it's not like they have chakras.

It's like they are chakras. In that way pure information can come to you moment by moment. As they change you can rapidly read what's going on because they are the mirror. [You read chakras.] just as you can read what's going on yourself in another person, however that person is relating to you.

Participant: Is chakra structure the same throughout the universe?

Elana: Yes and no, because it's constantly shifting until you come to the Neith. However there is a *consensuality* of access points that are the practices in the everyday world that they [the chakras] bring into the present. . . .

Seeing Aka

In the following exchange a participant reports seeing aka, not knowing at first what she is seeing.

Connie: If you look at rocks or earth you'll see –what's surprising—you'll see this aura . . .But then sometimes you'll see these little things shooting like this [gestures]. What's that?

Elana: The aka.

Connie: That is the aka?

Elana: Yes, that is the aka.

Participant: But it doesn't go anywhere.

Elana: That's the aka that's carrying the subtle energy. It's not that it doesn't go anywhere. It's that your vision doesn't take it any further than the point of its intensity. That is the point of intensity that is a chakra where subtle energy is entering the aka at a very high level, shall we say, at a place where there is a great quantity of it. Then it begins to dissipate into finer threads.

Connie: But do these akas go out to the connection [referring to aka fibers merging in a web connecting living beings.] and I only see it to a certain point?

Elana: You only see it to a certain point and as your vision develops you begin to see it as a web that is infinite.

Connie: If you look at something—I was looking at this rock and it looked like a mother whale and a baby. The mother whale just started to undulate in the center very much like it was alive. I've seen that in Hawaii up and down at the bottom of a volcano. The whole floor was undulating like it was . . . Then I was lying on the floor and the whole carpet started to undulate.

Elana: That's it.

Connie: But what is that?

Elana: That is when you are literally going beyond your barriers. You are literally going beyond the mind that has fixed reality. You're beginning to see the moving in all things.

A few minutes later Lisa asked, "Do you ever tell us a false story? "No." Elana said.

Like Little Children

Like dialogues between teacher and students in earlier sessions, the above dialogue strongly resembled a primary or kindergarten class. Participants had slipped into the roles of children once more, asking an adult to explain their experience of the world. My recordings and observations at mystery school show that participants often behaved in a childlike manner. They asked questions typical of kindergarten and grade school children, relating to Elana as if they were children and she was the all-knowing adult who explains the world. They had the sort of conflicts children have over depiction of gender roles and norms of social behavior. Needs usually repressed in Western adult social life such as those for immediate resolution, love and acceptance surfaced. Processing resembled tantrums. Participants displayed trepidation, frustration, and adventurousness.

In the West, a child's ego is not thought to be fully developed before the age of seven (Maier, H. W. 1978). During the years before seven the most intense, basic learning takes place, the primary acquisition of language and culture (Keesing 1981). Although an individual soon forgets experiencing this learning process, the behaviors and schema one has appropriated during the process remain internalized.

The mode of learning employed by Holakuna Mystery School participants corresponded to a child's learning. The participants were placing themselves, or allowing themselves to be placed in a tractable, trance state in which their adult ego function was subdued, hence their childlike behavior. The fact that participants frequently forgot much of what they had experienced during mystery school sessions (chapter 2) suggests that their learning was analogous to that of a small child who later forgets how she learned what she knows. Precepts learned at mystery school and forgotten later emerged in dreams, which then seemed precognitive.

Participants exhibited playfulness when they joked. Playfulness exemplified by the nurses' fashion show (chapter 2), threats of tickling Walt, and the discussion of dangers going out into the desert indicate participants were appropriating the Holakuna reality.

Play transforms the players, according to Paul Recour (1981). Entering a game, one gives oneself over to the space and the meaning being played. In this process what is known no longer constitutes everyday reality. Rather, everyday reality is suspended and a future offering new possibilities opens up. Mystery school participants in becoming playful abandoned themselves to the context of meaning that Elana provided, replacing their everyday reality with open possibilities. In moments of playfulness they were able to appropriate the essence of the Holakuna belief system and transcended their usual reality, learning in much the same way that children learn through play.

Archetypical figures (the neters) are, among other things, parental figures. Participants' interaction with neters, visualized in trance states, brought about a change in possibilities for relationships, possibilities appropriated during their infant and early childhood stages of bonding and learning, as well as later stages of adolescent or adult peer and pair bonding. These visualizations, combined with other mystery school activities had the power to alter participants' deep conceptualization of themselves in relationship to others.

The collaborative construction of the "holy family" created an environment of trust in which these processes could occur without threat. Truth and sharing circles enabled participants to reveal progressively more of their secrets to supportive peers in a climate of "non-judgment" and provided them with a cooperative, loving forum for dealing with past psychic trauma.

The Holakuna Mystery School implemented a collaborative process of appropriating the new system of knowledge as well as the reconstruction of participants' personal and social reality that appeared to reach deep levels of each person's unconscious mind. Most mystery school participants I interviewed noticed marked changes in their experience of reality (bi-location, synchronicities, being in the flow, increased therapeutic ability) as well as changes in the way others related to them. There were examples of perceived change in relationships. Nancy felt she had become aware of friends' covert emotions and was able to respond to these for the first time in her life. Kim said she had begun her first relationship with a man based on "affinity" and "bonding" rather than competition. Julie reported that close friends said she was "more relaxed and peaceful and more comfortable with who I am."

Chapter 8 Healing, Learning, and Transcending

Engulfed as Westerners are in our established scientific medical system, we forget that other cultures, particularly indigenous ones, have their own alternative medical knowledge of illness and treatment. For people in these cultures, as for most Westerners, the explanation of illness and treatment must resonate with one's deeply enculturated worldview in order to be satisfactory. (Hallowell 1963)

Nevertheless, indigenous medical practices in many societies have been influenced by outside cultural systems. Multiple systems present an array of therapies available, from which the afflicted may choose modes of healing consistent with their individual worldview. In the West during the 1980s there was a growing attraction to various kinds of "alternative" medicine. This same attraction led mystery school participants, many of whom were licensed healers, to study Holakuna alternative healing methods.

Holakuna Healing, Yoga and Shamanism

Beyond the eclectic "borrowing" common to human potential movement and new age groups, the marked similarity of the mystery school belief system with shamanic and yogic healing systems raises some questions. Is Holakuna basically yoga? Is its system of healing simply a combination of East Indian and shamanistic healing?

Holakuna and Yoga

Yoga teaches of shakti, the un-manifest universe which becomes manifest. Mind is a manifestation of shakti as force, which becomes matter in the form of five elements identical to the Holakuna elements. (Vishnudevananda 1960) Elana taught of the un-manifest void, and of mind and intention active in all forms of matter and energy. Yoga teaches of three bodies: the physical, astral, and causal bodies, derived from shakti, whereas Holakuna recognizes many such bodies. Yoga posits three levels of mind: (1) the subconscious, autonomic and instinctive mind, (2) the conscious intellect, and (3) the super-conscious higher mind, which achieves intuition. These three minds seem to correspond to the three selves of Holakuna. Yogic selves are two, the ego and atman.

Yoga also teaches of a form of energy, kundalini, referred to as serpent power, which resides below the root chakra and rises up through the spine to the higher centers when the chakras are opened. Kundalini yoga involves the upward movement of this shakti energy to unite with consciousness (Shiva) opening the third eye or ajna chakra and the thousand-petaled lotus, which is the seventh, or crown chakra. The raising of kundalini, effected through initiation and yogic practices, seems analogous to MS participants' journey through the chakras, and the work of the uraii (Huna energy serpents).

Mantra is the Sanskrit word, meaning literally 'tool of mind,' where the practitioner chants sounds, sacred words, or phrases by voice or focused silent thought, bringing human consciousness into vibrational alignment with higher states of being and awareness, resulting in transformation. Hence as yogis use Sanskrit mantras to invoke the powers of chakras, often visualized in the form of Hindu gods and goddesses, holakunas use ancient Egyptian mantras to change states of existence and to invoke the principles of neters.

The Sanskrit word for yoga means union. Long and continued practice of yoga, brings about the permanent union of kundalini with pure consciousness, the atman, which produces liberation from time, space and causation, followed by joy and bliss, (joy analogous to hunadity). (B.K.S. Iyengar 1976) Yogic teachings seem quite similar to Holakuna. Since I have not explicated yogic beliefs as fully as I have described Elana's Holakuna teachings in the preceding chapters, the analogy may be closer than depicted here.

There are, however, basic differences between the two disciplines. Hatha yoga centers on a naturalistic approach: proper diet, yoga exercises, and breathing practices. It is through breathing that yogis bring *pranic* energy into the body. Holakunas learn breathing practices similar to those of kundalini and kriya yoga, but Holakuna teachings emphasize subtle energy entering the etheric and physical bodies through the third eye or the crown chakra. They do not emphasize health and diet so much. Ashtanga yoga includes practices for purifying the body, abstaining from various foods, and limiting sexual activity. Elana taught that abstinence increases desire and firmly centers attention on the very appetite one wishes to subdue. Rather than abstain, she advised holakunas to indulge in their addictions until they became saturated and were ready to transcend the addiction. This approach has parallels with some practices of tantric yoga. Mystery school initiates sought to fully meet the physical and emotional needs of self and loved ones, valuing the physical and animal nature of humankind equally with the spiritual aspect.

In healing others, Vishnudevananda instructs healers to place their hands in the location of the patient's pain and imagine life energy moving from their hands to the affected area. (1960). This approach is analogous to beginning Huna healing techniques, although holakunas were instructed to hold their hands over the affected spot, not touching. Vishnudevananda also teaches that the yogi can mentally speak to the cells of the ailing body and command them to follow orders, since the cells have a mind. Elana taught that cells have mind and suggested that holakunas can carry on a dialogue with their cells in the same way that they can negotiate with microorganisms active in disease. Elana's system avoided hierarchy and "power over," even in regard to one's relationship with one's own cells.

According to *Yogini* Elizabeth Haich, Ayurvedic Medicine, a Hindu discipline with historic roots, recognized the appearance of diseases as spirit entities, personifying them as demons. Haich claims to have been told by such a physician (many years ago) that the form of each disease demon visualized by patients is consistent across cultures. The Ayurvedic physicians she consulted combated these spirits, rather than negotiating with them. (Haich: 1964)

Elana described for participants how the spirit of Candida appeared to her in a dream as a beautiful entity. Afterwards she was able to control her own Candida infection and to help other people control theirs. The Holakuna's attitude toward visualized disease entities is considerably more benign than that of Ayurvedic physicans depicted by Haich.

Holakuna and Shamanism

Holakuna also contains elements of shamanistic healing which may be incompatible with yogic thought. According to the shaman's traditional worldview most illnesses are caused by either flight of the soul or by a magical object introduced into the body by spirits or sorcerers. (Mirceau Eliade 1972; Winkelman 2000) The Shaman may remove the cause of an illness in the form of stone, feather, or some object, which he or she magically sucks out of the patient's body and disposes of (often by burying it).

Holakunas bury objects that have contained powerful spirits when they are no longer useful in order to restrain their power. For instance, when Shoshona's hand carved, spirit empowered gourd rattle was accidentally stepped on and smashed at mystery school, she asked Elana what to do with the remains. Elana instructed her to bury them, saying that otherwise Shoshona's low self would never believe the spirit was at rest.

In exorcism holakunas remove troublesome spirits from their clients' bodies only temporarily. They help their client reprogram a kha (in this case not the low self but a separate, possessing spirit or neural track), making it a helpful partner. Then practitioner and client return it to the client's unconscious.

Holakunas use various practices to protect themselves and others from attempts to drain their life force or steal their power. Shamans employ practices for the same reasons. Shamans and holakunas alike have spirit allies that protect and help them. In some societies spirits speak through shamans when they are in altered consciousness. In much the same way holakunas channel neters. Finally, the Holakuna notion of the significance and high status of animals is reified by Holakuna activities. Dancing the totem animal and putting on the animal head resemble shamanistic practices.

Participant Views of Holakuna Knowledge

Perhaps Elana's teachings seem to be a hodge-podge of yogic, shamanistic and new age elements, but my informants did not view them as such. They thought the Holakuna teachings amounted to an integrated system of knowledge. Before the sixth session of mystery school Rudolph commented, "It's not so much that Huna teaching is new, as that the format with which it's presented seems to be much more effective. It's just packaged in a way that seems to work quite well."

Julie saw Elana's teaching as "a body of knowledge, a lifetime learning" with one concept building on another. She said, "Elana is taking us through each chakra point, introducing us to that realm and giving us experience, ritual and empowerments at each chakra point." To participants the Holakuna system was a unified, independent discipline.

Maybe Elana constructed the whole system out of bits and pieces of other disciplines, including large selections from yoga and shamanism. If so, she did a masterful job. Although I'm sure that some of Elana's practices indeed were "borrowed" from these and other disciplines, and that such borrowing followed human potential movement eclecticism, I also assume that she had received specific esoteric knowledge from Marta and Albert. Elana herself implied that both yoga and elements of shamanism derive from the same ancient tradition of which Holakuna is a remnant, and that she had worked diligently to reconstruct as well as preserve these very ancient teachings.

Participant Learning Experiences

During interviews participants spoke of their experience appropriating the Holakuna belief system. They had differing views of how they internalized the teachings, but some general categories of ways of appropriating knowledge emerged.

Synchronicity: Being in the Flow

Experience with synchronicity was closely linked to participants' understanding of learning. Elana defined synchronicity as "meaningful coincidence,"[1] but her students had their own definitions. For Kim synchronicities just happened. She described two aspects of synchronicity:

> Events just seem to fall into place or varied events just seem to happen as if they're disconnected, yet they end up being totally connected. The other thing that I think of is being in the flow. That, to me, is being in tune with the rhythms of myself, which are natural rhythms of the universe so that things just easily flow.

On the other hand Regena and Ruth saw themselves attracting synchronicities by "putting out' their wants. This view connected synchronicity with manifesting. Regena reported:

> When I put out a need or circumstance that I want in my life it's just there. It just happens. Sometimes you wonder, "Why did it happen now when that's just what I want?" That happens on very small detail level as well as larger.

In the Barley Green incident Ruth said she "put out" a need in the form of sound, the spoken request. She told me: "Now that's what synchronicity is, putting it out, but it's through the medium, I feel, of the sound that it comes back. It may come back instantaneously, like it did for me."

Like holakunas, practitioners of yoga also report that synchronicities increase as an individual advances spiritually. One wonders whether coincidental events actually increase for these people, as they believe they do, or whether these spiritual practitioners just begin to attend to them. One thing is certain. With realization of the concept of synchronicity the meaning of each specific coincidence expands for a person. Each one is imbued with a new, deep meaning which seems to verify the rightness of or direction of the individual's course of action. This is partly because appropriation of any belief system introduces new concepts with their attendant symbolic meanings, so that everyday events take on deeper significance. This is one of the attractions of an alternative reality: new, richer meaning for life events. The power of the experience of synchronicity to bring about personal learning and change lies in meaning, not frequency.

Holakuna adherents experienced deeply meaningful interrelated coincidences occurring in both mundane and spiritual circumstances. "Simple things like something that's needed in the house," said Regena. "I want it to be on sale. Sure enough, the next paper I pick up, it's on sale. Of course Joe is one of the larger synchronicities." Regena maintained that she had manifested Joe, her husband.

Joe agreed, saying, "Circumstances were such that we got together. I'm not sure why that happened but it did. It seems very orchestrated, like it had to be that way."

Katherine spoke of numerous synchronicities leading up to her decision to begin seeking new employment culminated by an astrological reading that predicted a job change for her. Within hours after she made the decision, her superior called her in and said her position was being eliminated because of "corporate downsize."

Spiritual path synchronicities included visualizations and dreams as well as mundane events. Rudolph related, "Just as I was getting ready to begin mystery school this other group I've been involved with did some archetypical work and what came up for me was Isis and Osiris. Things like that keep happening." (Isis and Osiris were associated with the first weekend of Elana's mystery school.)

Elsa reported visualizations that were both precognitive and synchronistic. Her comments convey the deep personal meaning synchronicities provided for her:

I went on a Native American [weekend workshop] before mystery school. We had a ceremony to find our power animal. The power animal that I got is the same that Elana gave me. My power animal is a hawk. I always felt so attached to hawks and eagles. To me a hawk or an eagle is freedom. It's sort of a symbol of being free from this plane, a vision. Those kinds of animals can see really far.

An experience of synchronicity always involved learning, or at least confirmation of something already known or suspected. Elsa's experiences confirmed that her power animal was indeed a hawk, and that she should be studying Holakuna, just as Rudolph's indicated to him it was time to be involved with Egyptian neters. Katherine's perception of the need to change jobs was validated through a series of synchronistic events. If nothing else is learned, the experience of exceptional coincidence always validates the potency of synchronicity itself, as in Ruth's case when the Barley Green representative appeared.

Shoshona related a series of synchronistic events that confirmed her vocation as a shaman. She was working as a janitor at a school near Paloma. One evening while she was sweeping a classroom a large bird flew into a closed window and fell to the ground. She went outside, picked up the bird, and began doing Holakuna healing practices for it, thinking that it would "either revive, or it would die a very pleasant death." She noticed that it was some kind of hawk.

The bird revived, but it could not fly, so Shoshona called the local wildlife rescue league, whose staff instructed her to put the bird in a quiet dark place until she could bring it to their shelter. She found a box for this purpose in the school. Taking books out of the box she noticed one called *The Book of Merlin*. A drawing on the cover depicted Merlin the Magician with a unicorn, a badger, a hawk and other animals. Shoshona decided to borrow the book for a while. When she brought the bird to the animal rescue shelter, the staff informed her that it was a female merlin. She told me:

> I did not get the connection in that moment. The very next day . . .
> when I was out in the sunroom, I was going to sit down in a rocking
> chair and nurse my son. I sat down and I looked out the window. . . .
> The sun was rising and against the sun was a silhouette of the same
> kind of bird. As soon as I saw the bird I got the connections in a

flash of recognition: *female merlin, yes, myself. I have the capability. I am a female Merlin.*

That week Shoshona visited a friend who worked at Paloma. When the friend heard the story she brought out a dress somebody had left in one of the guest rooms, saying, "This is obviously yours." It was a long purple dress with the head of a hawk and the sun embroidered on the bodice. Shoshona was wearing it at the time of our interview. She said. "Oh, my wedding dress with my beloved, I wear it for all my ceremonies I do in town."

Learning Through Dreams

Practices taught by Elana and employed by the mystery school participants actively solicited dream learning. Most informants reported dreams of Elana teaching them in their sleep. Elsa said, "I've even had a dream of Elana teaching me how to breathe in a dream." Teachers other than Elana appeared in participant dreams when they were sought by a dream practice and when they were not. (Doing the practice did not insure that teachers would appear.) My dream of the two figures teaching me that the *so* is the source provides an example.

Many of these dreams seemed to anticipate coming mystery school lessons, as did Christy's dream of the giant insect that imparted streams of tiny skulls resembling the same ones Elana later handed out, and my dream of having a lion head, which occurred just before the weekend when we embodied the lion-headed goddess. These instances of precognitive learning through dreams are probably not as dramatic and

146

clear cut as they seem in the telling. A month or two after the "*so* is the source" dream, when I was going over tapes of previous mystery school sessions, I found that Elana had actually said the words "The *so* is the source" during lecture the first weekend. I had not remembered this at the time I had the dream. The dream seemed to predict the moving of the *so* practice we learned during the fifth weekend, but since Elana had previously mentioned that the *so* could be moved it was not an incredible prediction.

Elana's spiral curriculum presented the same material over from different points of view, often by means of metaphor and symbol. This promoted retention at a subconscious rather than a conscious level, and contributed to participants' sense that some dreams were precognitive of mystery school events. Still, there were unexplained precognitions in participant dreams as well as in synchronicities: for example Christy's dream of the giant insect imparting skulls. Dreaming was a means of learning for participants. Dreams that reinforced Holakuna precepts triggered powerful learning.

Learning as Remembering: Going Home

In addition to learning through dreaming, participants felt that mystery school was simply helping them remember information stored in their physical or their etheric bodies. Vanessa connected this process of remembering with synchronicity, saying:

> In synchronicity we are tapping information with a collective resident data bank. Somewhere "all having been" happens

simultaneously. Synchronicity means we get our ego out of the way so we can be here to perceive what's going on.

She also said:

At the deepest level what mystery school has to do with is remembering. That's what it's all about. There's some reservation or some acknowledging of the truth: of knowing oh, we've heard this story before. This is familiar. That's bigger than synchronicity. That's tapping into essential truth.

Regarding knowledge stored in the etheric body, Kim said:

I rediscovered knowledge I often already knew. . . . It comes back into my body. That's probably the trigger. . . . If I think of myself as an etheric body as well as this physical body, then my etheric body has vast amounts of knowledge and memory connected with it just from my own experience of the universal whole.

Participants also spoke of a sort of primal knowing for which they used the simple statement "I know."

Nancy said, "The teachings themselves are really a validation, a big validation of what I've known is true for my whole life."

Rudolph commented regarding his initial decision to attend the mystery school, "I had one of those hits, you know, that said, 'This is the one.' That's why I did it."

Elsa said, "I'll see an ad in the paper that I'm supposed to go somewhere like a spiritual event and I go. I have a feeling just from the ad that I should go and then it's confirmed."

Ruth asserted, "There's a part of me that's so deep that unless it rises from the depths spontaneously – almost everything that Elana says I already know. She'll take a certain hand position. I'll already know it. My body will already do it."

Cellular Learning

Holakunas not only believe that knowledge is stored in the body, but also that it is stored in individual cells. Vanessa said, regarding her decision not to make recordings or take notes at mystery school, "I believe that on some level it's recorded *cellularly*. I don't need to have a mountain of tapes and so forth."

Ann said, "We're learning at much more than the logical intellectual level. The learning is really occurring at a cellular level."

Participants articulated two different forms of cellular knowledge: rewiring the nervous system and DNA patterning. Ruth implied that human memory might be stored in and passed on with DNA when she spoke of her Hawaiian Kahuna teacher, saying, "She's called Lawna. It was in her childhood, her genetic pattern. I guess her mother, father or grandfather was Kahuna."

Katherine spoke at length about rewiring the nervous system:

If you visualize your nervous system itself, literally . . . all the nerve endings and all of that; it's a series of circuits. Then what I'm talking about is the circuitry being rewired. It's the initiations that accomplish this. That's where it's happening.

Participants believed that, as Elana had said, new neural tracks were

149

being formed by the initiations and the use of mantras and Holakuna practices. Participants would not be able to put concepts back in the same schema, i. e. "same old boxes."

Opening

There was general agreement that before one could learn in any of the above ways one had to open. Like bodies, opening also was described as either physical or etheric. Vanessa said, "My goal for myself is to come here as open and as present, so that I can take it all in." Later she said that she was learning by osmosis.

Katherine explained her understanding of opening:

When we keep ourselves as an open channel and recognize that the purpose of the ego is to help us individually: to help us to focus and move and function with this reality. But the ego needs to retain openness, an open channel because it's not who we are.

It's not only openness in terms of cosmic powers or whatever, but it's also maintaining openness with other people, to work with other people so that there's power in joining powers of people together to move forward.

Kim spoke of her personal experience of opening at another mystery school she had attended. She had a growing headache because she was holding throat energy. At length she felt her head was going to explode, so she went to the teacher. The mystery school teacher had her lie down, brought other people around, and started working on her head. The teacher told Kim to just let the energy flow, saying, "Open your crown chakra," to which Kim replied that it *was* open.

Kim told me, "I was still viewing myself as the container, so that as open as it could be was the diameter of my head."

The teacher told her, "Think of your head as the whole sky."
She continued:

> Suddenly I did and it was like I exploded. I was here and I wasn't here. In a way I knew my body was still here, but I literally physically felt like I was out for miles. I was myself but it was the most extraordinary feeling that I've had.

In this account opening constitutes a sort of letting go of learned cultural notions of the boundaries of self. Kim had transcended her limits, and learned through the experience that her self and her awareness were "part of everything."

Transcendence

The experience of transcendence Kim described exemplifies what mystery school participants sought. New age adherents wanted to transcend their acquired culture to reach a higher state of personal development. (Stone 1976) This idea of transcendence is known in theory of knowledge. The goal becomes what lies beyond or outside the person. To transcend is to step over. The transcendent is the one who steps over into something outside herself.[2] Participants not only sought to step over into the high self, the void, the neters, the interconnectedness of things, the universal truth, or even death; but to whatever they found beyond the limits of self as set by Western culture. To a greater or lesser extent they did transcend. These contemporary Hunas believed that it was not only possible, but important to extend human potential, and that they were leading the way. Why should they feel this need so strongly?

Notes

1. This is Carl Jung's definition (1971).

2. See Daya Krishna (1978) "Man According to Eastern Modes of Thinking," in Paul Ricoeur's *Main Trends in Philosophy*.

Chapter 9: Self, Mind and Revitalization

Journal Entries: April 7, 1989. It was a beautiful spring day and my daughter talked me into taking a walk in the country, a peaceful walk of a mile or two through a farm valley containing fields, forest lots, and country homes. On the way back, as we walked out of the valley, I looked back into it. Then I heard the harmony of the world singing within me. I was hearing and feeling this harmony and beauty of the world on this sunny spring day as a musical sound, a chorus of voices, singing a tone that was not quite "ah" and not quite "mmm." It was a blend of the two sounds in one.

When I heard the sound, I fell in love with the world. It was a physical sensation of bonding with nature, almost sexual. I understood then what Elana had meant when she told the mystery school that the joy of hunadity is like being in love. In the moment of hearing the tone, I "knew" that this state of joy was no fluke, but humankind's natural state, that people should always be hearing and feeling it. I realized that I had experienced this state and heard the tone before, especially when a child, but I had never been fully conscious of it as I was now. Mystery School had primed my awareness and given me the ability to hear the song and experience the joy of the world.

April 22, 1989. Today my friend from the coast came to visit and brought me a present. It is a little hand-made clay ocarina, oval in shape. On the top is impressed the Sanskrit symbol for *aum.* My friend did not know anything about Holakuna and I had not told her about my experience on April 7. The synchronicity was complete. I thought the universe was reminding me of my recent moment of hunadity.

Experiencing Holakuna Reality

The Holakuna Mystery School provided compelling evidence for what Berger and Luckman have called the social construction of reality. (1967) During my participant apprenticeship, I observed Elana and the mystery school students collaborate in constructing the Holakuna reality, and recorded participants' reports of their progress in experiencing it. Through mystery school each participant expanded his or her understanding of what is real and what is possible—physically, mentally or spiritually. For example: Carla saw a line changed on her palm; Katherine received a symbol from her neter; Connie saw aka.

Participants' appropriation of the alternate reality was highly individual. Each person brought a different background of spiritual or esoteric knowledge to mystery school. They appropriated different parts of the Holakuna belief system, according to their background and orientation. Thus Rudolph, who had spent nearly twenty years in "metaphysical work," said that "almost everything" Elana taught was familiar. He was praised for his channeling ability, but he had learned to channel years before he attended mystery school. Nevertheless he reported that the combination of powerful mantras and multiple rituals at Holakuna Mystery School was "very effective" for him. In conjunction with his Holakuna participation he observed things change in his life, including "becoming more assertive." Eventually he gave up smoking.

For Nancy, on the other hand, Elana's teachings were "brand new material." With no previous metaphysical experience, Nancy demonstrated a marked ability to channel on her first attempt. The highly individualistic outcomes of mystery school participation and the initiates' diverse backgrounds made it impossible to delineate a set of concepts which all participants appropriated there.

Attending the mystery school as a participant apprentice during graduate studies in anthropology and education, I became acutely aware of the cultural nature of the Western notion, and other notions, of self. I observed that the possibility and opportunity existed for Westerners to transcend the limits of the bound, unique, integrated, dynamic center of awareness, emotions, judgment, and action that has been identified as the Western concept of self. (Geertz 1973) Participants' bilocation and their experiences of hunadity exemplified this transcendence. I did not learn that the Holakuna notion of self is right and the Western notion wrong; rather I fathomed that the possibilities for definitions of self are broad, perhaps limitless.

Self

    Self is a culturally defined, learned perspective on being in the world (or out of it). The Western notion that a person is an independent thinking unit, bounded and separate can be attributed to Descartes and certain European thinkers of the seventeenth century, including Francis Bacon and Isaac Newton. It became a dominant view of science and model for interacting with "the world", depicted as a separate theater within which self is located.

    There are alternative points of view. (Gregory Bateson 1972, Morris Berman 1988: Susan Greenwood 2009) I do not deny the existence of individual human mind, sense of self, consciousness, and knowledge, but rather wish to point out that individual human genetic potential for awareness develops, is formed, within a particular culture or cultural mix. Development continues in adulthood. None of this discussion is new to anthropologists who have explored definitions of self in different cultures, but the implications for Western systems of knowledge, and therefore for education are enormous.

Mind outside Self

    We Westerners must consider the possibility that while humans, and at least some animals, have individual minds upon which they depend for survival, there are indications that mind also functions in the larger environment independently. Bateson (1972) spoke of circuits conveying information resulting in change in environmental systems. Drawing on cybernetics, he writes that any happenstance engaging causal circuits and a transmission of energy exhibits characteristics of mind. Such a system processes information and self-corrects. For Bateson, this constitutes mind. Following Bateson, the notion of separate logical selves, acting upon a world of objects, is dangerous. Humans, acting in disregard of a greater regulatory mind, may divert an entire ecosystem or society toward disequilibrium, uncontrolled runaway or entropy as opposed to natural balance.

The Urge to Transcend

Holakuna Mystery School participants attempted to transcend Western notions of the bounded separate individual self. Those I interviewed felt that if they could manifest their high self, they could influence Western culture in a positive way, as well as improve their personal situations. Julie spoke of Holakunas as shamans who were not engulfed in the mass consciousness, but who "Can move in and out of it at will and have the ability to remain united with the natural forces in an ancient lineage; (forces) that can work to restore balance wherever it (balance) is not."

Kim said, "What mankind is about is integrating the parts and together, rising to a higher level of consciousness." She explained that her experience of transcendence "took me to a different dimension and connected me with everything . . . . It in very subtle ways shifted dramatically what I thought about the world and myself."

The System Mind

In a belief system where mind is eminent in the social or ecological system rather than limited to the bounded sentient organisms, knowledge is the province of the system rather than the individuall.[1] The system itself transmits specific knowledge or a prompt, perhaps at the unconscious level, to an individual when he or she is needed to take part in a process that maintains or balances the system. Elements of the system, some of them human beings, may or may not be aware of the overarching mind, yet certain actions must maintain the system if it is to continue. To the extent that they are not aware of the purposes and operations of the system mind, a person performs the needed actions in either unconsciousness or false consciousness. False consciousness amounts to assuming they know what is going on and are in control, when in fact they do not and are not. Transcendence to a higher type of learning (ultimately wisdom) involves awareness above unconscious or false conscious participation.

Holakuna modes of learning and knowing: "opening," "I know," "Learning through dreams," "being in the flow," and "synchronicity" approach awareness of the system mind. A sentient informant living in the system may think:

There is a great body of knowledge surrounding me. Some of it resides with me so that sometimes I know without awareness of how I know. When I need to act in order to maintain balance, the

158

requisite knowledge may come through the system or through me. Either way, to receive that communication I must be in the flow of events. I watch for coincidences because they mark changes in the flow of events indicating needed knowledge is coming through. Sometimes I can tap into the integrated system mind. When I do, I identify with everything, and then my mind goes beyond myself, and I am changed.

This parallels what the mystery school participants like Kim, Julie and Regena told me. In a Batesonian universe, synchronicities may be viewed as communications from the system mind which will, if the receptor attends to them, maintain balance in the ecological, social, and personal system.

Revitalization

In 1924 linguist and anthropologist Edward Sapir delineated his conception of genuine culture. He emphasized the harmoniousness, balance and self-contained nature of this ideal, authentic cultural milieu. The genuine culture is rich and varied, but consistent and unified in attitude toward life, viewing each element that exists in relation to all others. Such a culture provides a worldview in which "nothing is spiritually meaningless" and in which "frustration, misdirection and unsympathetic effort" are conspicuously absent. (p. 410) Sapir added that every profound change in the flow of civilization (particularly change in its economic base) "tends to bring about an unsettling readjustment of cultural values" (p. 413).

Revitalization Movements

What anthropologists call a revitalization movement is one of the known human responses to the need for "unsettling readjustment of cultural values" and its attendant loss of spiritual meaning. In a well-known study, Anthony F. C. Wallace described a revitalization movement among the Iroquois Indians of New York State in 1799, which produced a new religion. (1966, 1970) With the British victory in the French and Indian War, the Iroquois were attempting to retain their customs and traditions, although these now seemed to bring only poverty and despair. Alcoholism was rampant.

A man named Handsome Lake, a Seneca Chief turned alcoholic, became seriously ill. In a death-like trance he experienced the first of several visions that lead to his recovery and the founding of a new religion. Quaker missionaries who were present when Handsome Lake revived from his trance and shared his vision recorded these events. Figures referred to in contemporary accounts as "angels" revealed principles of a new religion, combining the old native traditions with elements of cultural reform and providing a new moral code for the Iroquois. The Seneca embraced Handsome Lake's religion and through it achieved a remarkable revitalization of their culture.

Wallace has proffered the Handsome Lake religion as an example of a revitalization movement, which gives a people whose traditions and beliefs have been desolated the means to create a new, balanced cultural system. (1966) During the late 20th century some individuals responded to perceived imbalance in American culture by identifying with an alternative belief system. It might have been a traditional, new, or syncretic cultural alternative. (Meredith B. McGuire 1981)

A Revitalization Effort

Neither the Holakuna Mystery School nor Huna in general could be considered a movement, because of the limited field of its actions, and the individualistic appeal of the discipline to a very small subgroup in Western society. By definition a movement involves a much larger sector of society. Nevertheless the mystery school bore a resemblance to revitalization movements. I suggest it can be examined as a revitalization effort.

Holakunas were deeply concerned and frustrated about what they conceived to be the misguided belief system of Western culture. They sought and received guidance from dreams and visions, as well as from their high selves, through techniques introduced in mystery school. There were two aspects to the revitalization effort: Elana's teaching and participants' knowledge and experience in and out of the weekend sessions. The two aspects were not uniformly congruous given the varying backgrounds and esoteric knowledge participants brought with them. The participants expected Holakuna knowledge to provide a new approach to their personal lives and careers more effective than that acquired through their enculturation as children and youth, or their professional training. They actively sought to transform their notions of self and reality.

While the Holakuna belief system was not traditional, it was certainly new and syncretic. It combined features of belief systems that lie at the ancient and archetypical roots of Western culture: yoga, shamanism and ancient Egyptian religion, with the most avant-garde scientific thought. Many anthropologists believe that for the most part these ancient communal belief systems were more synergetic with their ecosystems than their modern Western counterparts. Early on mankind identified with the world around him and took that empathy as a guide for his own social organization and theory of psychology. (Bateson 1972; Darrell Posey 1983)

Crises in Meaning

I interpret Elana's teaching and the Holakuna Mystery School to be a revitalization effort in response to a crisis of meaning participants experienced in Western civilization. Both Elana and the participants spoke of certain perceived cultural situations that did not betoken an "inherently harmonious, balanced, and self-satisfactory system." These perceived situations had both global and personal significance.

Family and Societal Crisis

During the fourth weekend session Elana taught of family crises, including child birthing practices that precluded proper bonding within a system of child raising in which children were constantly "made wrong" by family members and thus could not develop sufficient self-esteem to function optimally as adults.

Participants discussed the prevalence of child and spouse abuse during session two, when they explored Western conceptions of gender. Most mystery school participants were acquainted with family crises, having encountered such cases in their professional work as counselors, therapists, nurses, or teachers and, for many, in their own families.

The themes of child or spouse abuse and contention about Western gender roles recurred in participant comments throughout mystery school. During the healing incident observed at the eighth weekend, Connie said Alice was an abuse victim, and prescribed healing for Alice and her family seven generations back. During these and other sessions participants also mentioned social crises including escalating violent crime, homelessness, and drug and alcohol addiction. Many of the family problems that surfaced during sharing and truth-telling sessions involved resolution of abusive or addictive situations.

Holakunas perceived that modern medicine failed to deal adequately with the spiritual, psychological, and social aspects of illness and death. This was hinted at in the nurses "fashion show." Elana, however, did not condemn the medical profession. She had found doctors who admitted they did not know what was wrong with her and conversed with her honestly. She said they were more helpful than "self–styled new age healers".

Environmental Crisis

Elana and the participants expressed concern about degradation of the world's environment through industrial pollution (from both products

163

and wastes), over-exploitation of natural resources such as timber and minerals, overpopulation, and exploitive agricultural practices. Elana believed that these situations directly contributed to prevalence of incurable diseases such as AIDS and some forms of cancer. She exemplified her concern over these situations in her lecture segment about curing a client's tumor by stepping between worlds.

At every session Elana raised the problem of Western attitudes toward nature, and especially the tendency to view animals as inferior entities or objects, placed at humankind's disposal. She especially emphasized this issue during the eighth session, when she taught that one must "put on the animal head" in order to reach the high self. A number of participants, including Carla and Lisa, spoke in favor of animal rights.

Predominance of War

Holakunas were concerned with the continuing threat of war, both nuclear war attended by the risks of nuclear preparedness, and meaningless wars in which the reasons for fighting and exactly who constituted the enemy were not clear (or all too clear). Elana depicted humankind's propensity for conflict as related to the modern understanding of gender roles. She considered war an unnecessary threat to the survival of humankind, related to the second chakra mind's fixation with dichotomies and hierarchies of power. Elana described this problem as worldwide, not just an aspect of Western society. Participants did not voice condemnation of war as strongly as Elana did, but their comments indicated that most of them shared her perspective on the matter.

Economic Crisis

Participants and Elana brought up their concern about economic crisis perceived in a social milieu in which homeless families in the United States survived on the streets and in parks, and in which increasing rents made maintaining a reasonable standard of living ever more difficult. They also discussed starvation, malnutrition, and general deprivations of the poor in third world countries in relation to the Holakuna teachings on the meaning of suffering.

Seeking Change

For mystery school initiates contemporary Western life and its basic belief systems did not provide a reasonable, logical, consistent system of meaning. Instead they saw it promoting the destruction of health, life and the environment, promulgating misery for life forms around the world. Holakunas sought a different belief system, one that promoted balanced, meaningful, satisfactory life for all creatures.

Participants' actions regarding employment provided evidence of crisis in meaning at the personal level. At least eighteen participants relied on independent practice or a self-owned business as a major means of support, indicating that employment with an existing organization did not meet their occupational goals or needs. Many of those not self-employed made job changes like Katherine's during the mystery school. They sought either a more meaningful job or a change of assignment in which they expected their talents to be better appreciated and used.

Katherine, Elsa, Rudolph, Ann, Julie, Kim, Ron, Virginia, Nancy, Jill, and at least one other participant made such changes.

Participants' concern with healing is also a key to their disenchantment with Western belief systems. They envisioned themselves healing not only their physical bodies, but also their social and material environment, perceiving these to be linked. The restoration of health and meaning for one ill person could restore order and meaning for the entire social group. (McGuire 1988) Elana told participants that if they could not make peace and resolve gender conflicts within the mystery school, it could not be done in the world. Regina said of humankind:

> All of their selves have the knowledge of their belief systems. Their whole being puts out the frequency that is sometimes called their signature. Whatever they're putting out is what they get back. You can direct that to get what you want in your life and to change the negative patterns that are getting things you know won't work . . . to make changes on the physical, mental, spiritual, emotional levels.

> Maybe some of the bigger things that happen in the world are due to the mass consciousness, the mass vibration. These things happen because of the frequency of the masses. So it is happening on an individual level but it's also happening on a small group level, bigger group level, world level.

Regena implied that changing the "frequencies" at the individual and group level could bring about mass changes.

Ann said, "If we change and we're willing to go into the darkest part of ourselves, somehow that will carry over to the rest of the world."

Participants viewed Western culture itself as "sick" and in need of healing, and they expressed a desire to find ways to ameliorate the conditions listed above. Regarding revitalization movements, Wallace wrote that when individual prophets and their followers regenerate spiritually, a real change in society may come to pass. Even when it doesn't happen, the devout believe it possible. (1966)

Is Holakuna a Religion or Cult?

Religion is difficult to define; there is no generally accepted definition among social scientists. Wallace maintains that the defining characteristic of religion is the premise that souls, supernatural beings, and supernatural forces exist (1966).[2] Critics of this view point to Taoism, which does not seem to contain any such premise; supporters of it reply that Taoism is a philosophy, not a religion. Religious behavior and beliefs seem to encompass an area of culture which is also the territory of "belief system" and "metaphysics."

The mystery school version of Huna lacked a collective dimension and certain accoutrements typical of Western religions and cults. There were no regular prayer meetings or formulated repetitious rituals, no distinctions between clergy and laity, no "musts" or "must nots," no duality between good and evil, and no clear demarcation of profane from sacred in the Holakuna belief system. I recognized that some of these features might develop within Holakuna in the coming years.

Elana's insistence that participants come to agreement on simple daily decisions such as "When should we have lunch?" her reticence to stop participants from asking Sally to leave mystery school, her denigration of "making wrong" and "power over," and her openness in sharing her own feelings of frustration and failure to communicate with participants all served to keep her out of the role of guru. Yet it was difficult to predict whether she could continue to avoid becoming a guru in the future.

Regena attended Elana's memorial service in 1999. She told me that during the reading of a poem about Elana at the memorial some of Elana's followers repeated the last line of each stanza together, chanting "She was our God."

Notes

1. Here I am indebted to Professor C. A. Bowers for suggesting applications of Bateson's theory of system mind to education.

2. See Keesing (1981).

Glossary

Akasha or akasa. One of the five elements. The element that both dissolves and contains everything else.

Ancestors. An individual's genetic ancestors for at least seven generations back who are present in their DNA. Isis and Osiris, neters of South, earth, body, love. The stars or beings that came from the stars.

Aura. A field of subtle energy which holakunas sometimes perceive surrounding living things.

Chakras. Seven subtle energy vortexes located in the body along the spinal column. In Holakuna chakras are considered separate minds.

Channeling. A process through which a person in trance makes known a communication from a spirit entity, a neter, or the high self, usually by direct speech of the spirit voice through the person's vocal apparatus.

Dismemberment. Refers to the shamanistic vision of being dismembered and put back together by spirits or gods in a way that increases shamanistic powers. Sometimes described as a Kundalini energy crisis, a condition in which chakras open spontaneously in an individual accompanied by symptoms of mental illness. A sudden falling away of meaning in life followed by acquisition of new, inspirational meaning. Changing established neural tracks.

Dream Teachers. Teachers, known or unknown, who appear in dreams and impart knowledge or wisdom.

Elements. What Hunas call elements westerners might refer to as states of matter-energy. They are earth (solid matter), fire (energy, heat), water (liquid), air (gaseous, ethereal), and akasha or akasa (dissolves and contains all).

Emotion. Emotion is thought by Holakunas to be a kind of energy which flows through the body and between individuals. Emotional blocks are located in the physical body and need to be cleared or released for the individual to function optimally. These can be but are not always khas.

Etheric Bodies. Spiritual energy bodies not usually visible to the human eye. Holakunas recognize at least ten such bodies per individual.

Harmonic Convergence. On August sixteenth and seventeenth of 1987, according to new age author José Arquelles' interpretation of the ancient Mayan calendar, earth entered a beam from space 5,125 years in diameter, heralding the beginning of a new era of interplanetary communication and spiritual union (Arquelies 1987). On those days 144,000 people were to go out on hills and mountains in groups or singly all over the planet to greet the dawn and create a field of trust. Thousands of people in the United States did go out to greet the sunrise, although it is doubtful the critical number was reached worldwide.

High Self. One of the three major divisions of the human self. The source of the divine, or God within the human being. Divinity existing as a major part of a human being.

Holakuna. A name for the mystery school teachings that the author made up to protect the identity of the mystery school and its participants. Also applied to initiates in the teachings. Elana could not legally use the terms huna or kahuna.

Huna. The name of a purportedly ancient, secret tradition passed down from predynastic Egypt. The word "huna" is said to be a Hawaiian term literally translated hidden treasure or treasure within. The term also refers to practitioners of Huna (including the Holakuna Mystery School participants) and is used as an adjective.

Hunadity. A state of joy, ascension, inseparability of all things, learning through living, living in the moment, and supernal regeneration.

Kha or ka. A complex, habit, or invading spirit, usually acquired in early childhood or in a previous incarnation. Some khas limit an individual's possibilities for self-development because they cannot easily be changed or redirected. The low self is made up of khas.

Kahuna. Commonly known as a term for a Hawaiian priest or shaman. Also used in surfer jargon of the 1960s on the West Coast of America referring to a "big man" in surfing. In the Hawaiian language a term for a priest, sorcerer, magician, minister, healer, or expert in any field. Hunas regard this term as the name of the Hawaiian Huna tradition which they believe was kept alive in Hawaii by a secret society within the native priesthood.

Low Self. In Huna thought, one of three major divisions of the human being. The low self includes the unconscious mind, body awareness, and the autonomic nervous function.

Manifesting. Bringing desired material objects and opportunities into one's life through Holakuna practices combining emotion, visualization and direction of subtle energy.

Middle Self. One of the three major divisions of the human individual, corresponding to the ego plus the persona of Jungian psychology. The logical, thinking, time bound part of a person active in the mundane world.

Neters. Ancient Egyptian archetypes commonly called gods, but regarded by holakunas as principles or forces operating in the world, personified in society, and functioning in the mundane world of socially defined reality.

Power Animal. A species of animal symbolizing or encapsulating the individual holakuna's low self, also referred to as the individual's totem animal. The term "power animals" can refer to additional animals which are spirit allies of the Holakuna practitioner.

Processing. Mystery school participants' term for a spontaneous "acting out" of emotional blocks they were working through. Processing involves one or more of the following overt behaviors: screaming, groaning, crying, gagging, vomiting, flailing limbs, and rolling on the floor.

Psychic surgery. Surgery done on the etheric body by means of subtle energy directed through the hands or third eye of the practitioner. Since the etheric bodies interpenetrate the physical body, psychic surgery often involves ethereal penetration into the physical body.

Re-membering. A process of going back in time mentally, disassembling events of past history and putting them together in a new way. Changing the body's DNA.

Seeing. Perception, usually visual, that goes beyond what is commonly considered the normal range of the senses, as in perceiving the aura, spirits, visions, and events and organisms in close, distant or future settings. Seeing is done with the third eye (the sixth chakra).

Shabin. Metaphorical dragons. The juncture of telepathic agreement and of opportunity.

So. The *so* is the center of being. A doorway within the body usually located at the solar plexus. The still point.

Spirit. The essence or nature of the universe expressed in three simultaneous processes: creation, preservation and destruction. The vibration that lies behind matter and energy, or its source. The word.

Stuff. A term employed by mystery school participants to mean complexes or khas and accompanying emotions that they were trying to reprogram, or work through.

Synchronicity. A Jungian term that mystery school participants used to describe the way they perceive fortuitous events and learning opportunities cropping up in their lives in conjunction with symbols or themes related to their self-development. Meaningful coincidence. A signal from the high self.

Third eye. The sixth chakra located between and slightly above the eyes. It is associated with clairvoyance and all types of psychic seeing, as well as psychic communication.

Uraii. Metaphoric snakes representing subtle energy.

Ush. The void.

References

Allison, Ralph B., M. D. with Ted Schwarz

  1999 Minds in Many Places: Revealing the Spiritual Side of
  Multiple Personality Disorder. Paso Robles, CA: CIE
  Publishing.

Arguelles, Jose

  1987 The Great Return, Interview by John Alexis Viereck.
  Meditation. Summer 1987/ 7-19, 50.

Bandler, R., and John Grinder

  1981 Trance-Formations: Neuro-Linguistic Programming and
  the Structure of hypnosis. Moab UT: Real People Press.

  1982 Reframing: Neuro-Longuistic Programming and the
  Transformation of Meaning. Moab, UT: Real PeoplePress.

Bateson, Gregory

  1972 Steps to an Ecology of Mind. New York: Ballentine Books.

Beckford, James A.

  1985 the World Images of New Religious and Healing Movements
  In Sickness and Sectarianism: Exploratory Studies in Medical
  and Religious Sectarianism. Ed, R. Kenneth Jones Pp. 72-93.
  Brookfield, VT: Gower Publishing Company.

Berger, P. L., and Thomas Luckmann

  1967 The Social Construction of Reality. NY: Doubleday.

Berger, P. L.

  1969 A Rumor of Angels. Garden City, NY: Doubleday.

Learning the Mysteries

Learning the Mysteries

Berman, Morris
1988 The Reenchantment of the World, Toronto, New York: Bantam Books.

Capra, Fritjof
1984 The Tao of Physics. New York: Simon and Schuster.

Castaneda, Carlos
1968 The Teachings of Don Juan. New York: Simon and Schuster.

Clarke, Arthur
1953 Childhood's End. New York: Ballantine Books.

Easthope, Gary
1985 Marginal Healers. *In* Sickness and Sectarianism: Exploratory Studies on Medical and Religious Sectarianism. R. Kenneth Jones, ed. Pp. 52-71. Brookfield, VT: Grover Publishing Company.

Eisler, Riane
1987 the Chalice & the Blade: Our History: our Future. San Francisco: Harper and Row.

Eliade, Mircea
1972 Shamanism: Archaic Techniques of Ecstasy. Princeton, NJ: Princeton University Press.

Foltz, Tanice
1985 Alternate Healing Group as a New Religious Form: TheUse of Ritual in Becoming a Healing Practitioner. *In* Sickness and Sectarianism: Exploratory Studies in Medical and Religious

176

Sectarianism. Ed R. Kenneth Jones. Pp. 144-157. Brookfield, VT: Gower Publishing Company.

Goodman, Felicitas D.

1988 Ecstasy, Ritual and Alternate Reality: Religion in a Pluralistic World. Bloomington and Indianapolis: Indiana University Press.

Greenwood, Susan

2009 The Anthropology of Magic. New York: Berg.

Haich, Elizabeth

1964 Initiation. Palo Alto, California: Seed Center:

Hallowell,A. I.

1963 Ojibwa World View and Disease. *In* Man's Image in Medicine and Anthropology. I. Goldstone, ed. Pp. 258-315. New York: Institute on Social and Historical Medicine, Academy of Medicine, International Universities Press.

Houston, Jean

1987 The Search for the beloved: Journeys in Mythology and Sacred Psychology. Los Angeles: J. P. Tarcher, Inc.

1982 The Possible Human: A Course in Enhancing Your Physical, Mental, and Creative Abilities. Los Angeles: J. P. Tarcher.

Iyengar, B. K. S.

1976 Light on Yoga: Revised Edition. New York: Schocken Books.

Jung, Carl

1971 Aion: Phenomenology of the Self. (From Aion:

Researches into the Phenomenology of the Self.) Collected Works, (Vol. 11, pars. 1-42) *In* the Portable Jung. Ed. Joseph Campbell translated by R. F. C. Hull. Pp. 139-162. New York: The Viking Press.

Keen, Sam
1988 Faces of the Enemy: Reflections of the Hostile Imagination. San Francisco: Harper and Row.

Keesing, Roger M.
1981 Cultural Anthropology: A Contemporary PerspectiveSecond Edition, New York: Holt, Rinehart and Winston.

King, Serge
1985 Mastering Your Hidden Self: A Guide to the Huna Way. Wheaton, IL: The Theosophical Publishing House.

Kloss, Jethro
1975 Back to Eden. Santa Barbara, Ca: Woodbridge Publishing Company.

Krishna, Daya
1978 Man According to Eastern Modes of Thinking. *In* Paul Ricoeur, Ed. Main Trends in Philosophy. New York: Holmes and Meier Publishers

Leadbeater, C. W.
1980 The Chakras. Wheaton, Il: The Theosophical Publishing House.

Llewelyn-Davies, Melissa
 1981 Women, Warriors, and Patriarchs. In Sherry B. Ortner &
     Harriet Whitehead, Eds. Sexual Meanings, the Cultural
     Construction of Gender and Sexuality. New York: Cambridge
     University Press.
Long, Max Freedom
 1981 Mana or Vital Force: Selections from Huna ResearchBulletins:
     Cape Girardeau, Missouri
MacDonald, Jeffrey L
 1995 Traditions for the New Age: A Case Study of the Earth
     Energy Tradition. Anthropology of Consciousness 6(4):31-45.
Maier, H. W.
 1978 Three Theories of Child Development. New York: Harper and
     Row.
McGuire, Meredith B.
 1988 Ritual Healing in Suburban America. New Brunswick:
     Rutgers University Press.
 1981 Religion: The Social Context. Belmont, CA: Wadsworth
     Publishing Company.
McGuire, Meredith B., and Debra J. Kantor
 1987 Belief Systems and Illness Experiences: The Case of non-
     Medical Healing Groups: Research. In The Sociology of
     Health Care, (6):221-248.

Morrell, Rima A.

2005 The Sacred Power of Huna. Inner Traditions: Rochester, Vermont.

Pavio, Allan

1986 Mental Representations: A Dual Coding Approach. Oxford University Press: New York.

Pinch, Geraldine

1994 Magic in Ancient Egypt. Austin: University of Texas Press.

Posey, Darrell

1983 Indigenous Ecological Knowledge and Development of Amazonia In Delema of Amazonian Development.Emilio F. Moran, ed. Pp. 225-258. Boulder, CO: Westview Press.

Ricoeur, Paul

1978 Main Trends in Philosophy. New York, London: Holms and Meier Publications, Inc.

Sapir, Edward

1924 Culture, Genuine and Spurious. American Journal of Sociology 29(1924):401-429.

Stone, Donald

1976 The Human Potential Movement In The New Religious Consciousness. Charles Glock and Robert N. Bellah, eds. Pp. 93-115. Berkeley: University of Califonia Press. 152. New York: Seabury Press.

Townsend, Joan B.

    2004 Individual Religious Movements: Core and Neo-
        Shamanism. Anthropology of Consciousness 15(1):1-9.

Vishnudevananda, Swami

    1960 The Complete Illustrated Book of Yoga. New York: Bell
        Publishing Company.

Wallace, Anthony F. C.

    1966 Religion: An Anthropological View. New York: Random
        House.

    1970 The Death and Rebirth of the Seneca. New York: Alfred A.
        Knopf.

Wallis, Roy

    1985 Betwixt Therapy and Salvation: The Changing forms of the
        Human Potential Movement. *In* Sickness and Sectarianism:
        Explorative Studies in Medical and Religious Sectarianism. R.
        Kenneth Jones, ed. Pp 23-50. Brookfield, VT: Gower
        Publishing Company.

Winkleman, Michael

    2000 Shamanism: The Neural Ecology of Consciousness and
        Healing. Westport, Connecticut: Bergan & Garvey.

Yogananda, Paramahansa,

    1998 Autobiography of a Yogi. Los Angeles, CA: Self
        Realization Fellowship.

Acknowledgements

I wish to expresses my sincere appreciation for the late Professor Harry F. Wolcott's continued encouragement and support for the initiation of my research as well as for the preparation of this retelling, and for the late Professor Richard Chaney's counsel. Mariah Nash Hencke, Professor Heewon Chang, and Karen Koppenhoefer's continued encouragement is also greatly appreciated. I thank Professor Aletta Biersack, for her advice, and Professor C. A. Bowers for sharing his insights. I owe a great deal to Elana and Regena, my Huna teachers, for agreeing to and advocating for the original study and to Karin Welsh who provided an excellent edit of the current manuscript, including her expertise regarding the section on yoga. Diane Hogan contributed a very helpful reader's critique. Finally I thank my interviewees and all the mystery school participants who made this book possible through their acceptance and cooperation.